To Cheryl,

A fellow pilgrim on

Earth's journey

Encouraging Words
for All Seasons

Iris Lee Underwood

Iris Lee Underwood

Sep. 17, 2006

HATS
OFF™

Published by Hats Off Books™

601 East 1st Street
Tucson, Arizona 85705 U.S.A.
www.hatsoffbooks.com

International Standard Book Number: 1-58736-016-0
Library of Congress Card Number: 00-109675

Cover art by Andrea Kaiser
Illustrations by Cherie Meyers and Andrea Kaiser
Cover and book design by Atilla Vékony

Printed in the United States of America

To Becky, Kelly and Ruth

Acknowledgements

With great pleasure I thank Brad Kadrick, former editor of the *Oxford Leader* in Oxford, Michigan, for seeing the need for encouraging words in his newspaper. Thanks, Brad, for giving me a voice in my community, for giving me my first break as a writer. Thanks for taking me under your wing and guiding me into the writing world. Maralee Cook, thank you for taking up where Brad left off. You were a marvelous mentor. And my considerate friend, Martha Chaffee, thank you for typing one third of this book.

Sadie McCoy, my mother and favorite storyteller, this book wouldn't be half of what it is without you. Linda, Libby, Patty and Sonia, my beloved sisters (in birth-order), thank you for believing in my writing talent and providing an interesting family to write about.

Friends and neighbors, co-workers and other individuals named in the following essays on encouragement, thank you for opening your life to the public.

Last, but certainly not least, Mel, Becky, Kelly and Ruth, thanks for your permission to publish our private lives for residents of Oxford, Michigan, and Matewan, West Virginia, to read.

My deepest gratitude to all of you for granting me the pleasure and privilege of making a dream come true.

Iris Lee

Prologue

To everything there is a season, and a time to every purpose under heaven… (Ecclesiastes 3:1)

This book is about finding encouragement in all seasons of life, particularly in mid-life and the empty nest. Friends, enemies, books, poetry, movies, letters, nature, prayer, and a multitude of other encouragers cross our paths daily. Many we recognize, others we do not.

But our eyes can learn to discern encouragement in the most unusual and unexpected places. If we close our natural eyes to see with our spiritual eyes, if we keep the eyes of our souls open, fear and failure will diminish. Why? Because we have embraced courage.

This is precisely when we see our destiny clearly before us, daring to dream our dreams. Then comes the thief to rob us of our treasure. Yes, courage is a treasure easily taken from us. But if we have eyes to see, the great gift of encouragement is certain to pass before us once again.

A wise heart opens wide to see and receive the goodness and mercy bound in the essence of encouragement. It is this power of observation that revives joy and courage at our lowest ebb. It is the intake of the fresh breath of truth that awakens our heart to see our purpose, to believe in our purpose, to fulfill our purpose. A positive energy then flows from us with such infectious force that the diseases of the mind, heart, soul and body are healed. We become agents of courage. Agents of inspiration. Agents of desire.

That is how this book happened. The marriage of inspiration and desire produced my weekly column,

"Encouraging Words," for a local newspaper. The following pages are filled with images and legacies of encouragement, written with the intention to cause the human heart to embrace faith, hope and love.

Enjoy the journey as we begin chronologically with the first of my published essays in September 1995 to the last printed in November 1998. The following pages contain songs of encouragement from a mother's heart—a heart passing through the seasons in life. Seasons of hope and despair, faith and fear, joy and depression, love and hate, and birth and death.

Iris Lee Underwood

Seasons

September 27, 1995

The changing of seasons brings exactly that—change. Not only the earth experiences transition from one purpose to another, but we inhabitants do as well. Seasons force upon us the inevitable and perpetual turning from hot to cold, green to white, sowing to reaping: turn, turn, turn.

For me, fall offers the greatest challenges of all seasons. It marks the end of my favorite season, and the introduction to my least appreciated. I've been making serious efforts to change my attitude and learn to enjoy the refreshing offerings of fall before the cold isolation of winter arrives.

My ambivalence to change was challenged last fall. I found myself headed for the uncharted season of the empty nest. I had planned and prepared for this passage, and now I was standing at the door.

What was I going to do with the rest of my life? I had always worked part-time, but my heart's desire was to pursue a writing career. After great thought and discussion with family and friends, I decided to return to school to develop and polish my writing skills.

Reluctantly, I resurrected my transcripts of 26 years. They need such things for college registration. Anxiety flushed through me as I took another look at my grades. Bad, just plain bad.

It was going to take a great deal of humility to surrender this to a stranger. I felt like a failure. Did I really want to return to school? Was it worth the exposure?

I stood at the desk in the counseling office, explaining my intentions. When the secretary asked for my transcripts, I handed them over, feeling like an embarrassed school girl. Wanting to defend myself, I muttered a remark about my poor grades. How could she know about my parent's divorce during my senior year in high school and the mess my mind was in when I left home for Central Michigan University in 1968?

The secretary returned a smile and said, "Yes, but you aren't the same person today you were then."

Her words were sincere and spoke truth to me. My shame was overwhelmed with the reality that everyone experiences failure, and failure is not fatal.

As I left the building, her words continued to encourage me. I wondered how many middle-aged spirits she had lifted with her kindness and understanding. I thought how she certainly was in the right place to promote education.

She helped me realize it was not my time for a college education 26 years ago. My time is now.

You see, dear reader, every season has its purpose, and thanks to the Oakland Community College secretary, I am going to enjoy my season of higher education.

Fresh Water

October 4, 1995

I wiped the blurring tears from my eyes as I stopped my car close to the mailbox. The country road covered the parched flowers planted in my old black porcelain canner with dirt. With a deep sigh I thought, I don't even have the energy to carry my watering can to the road to water my dying flowers.

I was exhausted — limp from the day's work and the fight to keep the tears locked inside my head. But the strength of sorrow defeated my efforts. I was crying again at the memory of my dad.

I scolded myself for not "getting over" his death sooner, and questioned why I was powerless over the gripping grief. I quickly scanned the mail while attempting to compose myself. I smiled when I found a letter from Dotty, a faithful friend from Massachusetts.

My family was in the kitchen when I opened the door. We exchanged greetings and I sat down to read Dotty's note. Dotty had priority to preparing dinner. She responded to the news of my dad's death. Her words were designed for my state of mind and heart. She wrote, "God knows my strength and has never asked me to face what you have faced. He knows how strong you are. Please remember, I will always be here for you whenever you need me."

I disagreed with her self-analysis. I met Dotty in Michigan years ago before she suffered abandonment when her husband left her with four children under the age of eight. She returned home to Massachusetts and raised her children with no support of any means from her husband. All four graduated from college by Dotty's pure grit. Never have I had to face such crisis. In my eyes, Dotty is the example of strength.

I sat holding her note in my hand, reminiscing her trials and courageous history. My daughter noticed my tears and tenderly asked, "It's about Grandpa, isn't it?"

I nodded "yes," and shared with deep emotion the encouragement Dotty had offered me. She renewed my courage to face the grief, and the strength to cry. If she believes I am strong enough to overcome my losses, then I must be. I could trust the judgment of a champion over-comer.

The next day I filled my watering can, walked to the road and poured fresh life over my flowers. Just like me, they were revived.

Inch by Inch

November 1, 1995

The spring weather was perfect for the 1993 Macomb County track and field meet. Ruth, my youngest daughter, was competing in the high jump. We were pleasantly surprised with her success as a sophomore in this field event. We had ten accumulative years of cross-country and track meets under our belts, but our girls had never competed in field events. This was a new frontier.

We fans leaned against the fence that separated us from the field, forming a line of cheering supporters. The intensity grew each time Ruth cleared the bar, and each time the bar was raised. I took a picture of her at each new height, not knowing if that jump would be the last.

But she kept on jumping and clearing the bar. The contest was down to a duel.

The bar was raised again. I trembled with tension as I tried to steady the camera. She missed her first of three possible jumps. My heart exploded.

That's okay, I thought, she has two more jumps. She can do it!

We yelled our vote of confidence to Ruth. As I wondered how she was handling the stress, one of her team mates, Andy, looked at me and jokingly said, "Ya know, if they would only lower the bar for Ruth, she could jump it and put an end to this so we could go home."

I laughed some of the tension out of my body while the camera continued to shake in my hands. Like crows lined up on a fence, we cawed our cheers of support as we watched Ruth win the championship title.

Andy's absurd recommendation has played back in my mind on many occasions. His sense of humor reminds me how ridiculous it is to abandon a goal just because we miss our first or second jump.

I'm sure the thought of lowering the bar never entered Ruth's mind. That's not how the contest works. Why would she return to heights she had already mastered? Her goal was to stretch herself with every added inch.

Don't we all sometimes want to lower the bar in our high jumps of life? When the going gets rough, we want to return to the familiar, the comfortable.

But let's remember Ruth and the exhilaration of victory. Let's remember Andy and laugh in the face of stress. And remember, goals aren't achieved overnight and champions aren't made in a day.

We reach new heights jump by jump and inch by inch.

Catch a Falling Star

November 29, 1995

I left the confines of Oakland Community College's building D at 9 p.m. on October 12, 1995, and walked into a galaxy gazing spectacular. Ah, the warm, autumn season. Yes. I would treat myself to some stargazing in my backyard.

My husband, Mel, joined me as we spread one of Granny's quilts on the ground. With our bed pillows in place, we lay down and covered ourselves with another blanket. Focusing on the sky, we agreed this could be our last opportunity this fall to share such an evening.

Mel was pleased to find the Little Dipper. I told him I hadn't seen a falling star in years, and would love to see one. He told me he had seen several lately. I was envious.

Then it happened. A falling star streaked across the sky, creating an aura of awe which fell upon us like inspirational stardust. We marveled at the timing—that our eyes were looking at *that* piece of sky at *that* second to see this miracle.

We wondered how many miles the star traveled during the half-second of its glory. Two more stars fell for an encore.

We embraced the stars until we chilled from the cooling, moist night air. As we entered the house, I started singing:

"Catch a falling star, and put it in your pocket. Never let it fade away. Catch a falling star, and put it in your pocket. Save it for a rainy day."

The archived song was resurrected by the timeless message of the falling star: Mel and I need to take time to stargaze. We must avail ourselves for inspirational moments that enrich our lives: to take time to ponder the greatness of God's creation. Those moments are resources

11

for the cloudy and starless nights: a reserve of stardust to sprinkle over our hardships and enlighten our lives.

I'm learning to use my starlight instead of dwelling on problems. I'm singing with Perry Como, and Mel and I are dancing to his mellow voice:

"For love may come and tap you on the shoulder some starless night. Just in case you feel you want to hold her, you'll have a pocket full of starlight."

Mel and I didn't have to travel to a foreign country to find beauty, adventure and intimacy. On a scale of 1 to 10, the romantic in me would rank our falling star a 10, next to our sunny May morning together in Paris's Luxembourg gardens. (Mel says he wouldn't go that far.)

The way I see it, we have the heavens above our heads and the Underwood Gardens beneath our feet, just waiting to offer us the wonder they possess. Our only cost is our time, and the desire to catch a falling star.

Al's Message

December 6, 1995

Al and Lil hired me several years ago as a housekeeper because emphysema had weakened Lil and rendered her dependent upon oxygen.

Both retired, Al lovingly cared for Lil, but couldn't keep up with the house. Within the year, after she had wormed her way into my heart, Lil died suddenly.

Al greeted me as a good friend when I offered my sympathy at the funeral home. Standing by Lil's casket, he spoke adoring words about his "bride" as his deep, sensitive blue eyes expressed his devotion and sorrow. I felt honored to share his suffering.

I was glad to accept Al's offer to retain my services. I wanted to maintain our friendship and check on his welfare. Since he's a man of few words, I asked questions.

We talked about our fears and this crazy world. He became my senior advisor and dear friend. He meets with his buddies daily at the local McDonald's to discuss the world's problems and shares a summary with me on my cleaning days. Their point of view makes a great deal of sense. These are the dying breed of World War II vets who think wisely, talk plainly and live simply.

Last December, I was cleaning Al's house when he was out on an errand. Christmas was closing in on me, and I was nowhere near ready. I was feeling the pressures of the holidays.

Noticing the obvious absence of Christmas decorations in Al's house, I felt sorry for him. He had previously told me he didn't want to bother with a tree.

I couldn't imagine *no* festivities during the holidays. No smell of cookies baking. No Christmas dinner. No Christmas concerts. No twinkle lights.

When Al arrived, he related the following incident: He had taken some items to Dominican Sisters distribution center, FISH. As he was waiting his turn to donate, a young mother with three small children unloaded a van full of new toys for contributions. Al perceived the mother as cheerful who managed herself and her children with an attitude of giving.

With his trademark teary eyes he said, "It did my heart good to see a young mother with three little kids make a sacrifice for those who aren't as fortunate. I'll tell ya, Iris, I got a lump in my throat." I could hear the effects of the lump.

Yep, I felt mighty foolish. Al had it right all along. When was the last time I felt a genuine lump in my throat from baking fruitcakes and cookies, Christmas shopping, decorating a tree or wrapping presents?

In my efforts to make the mood of Christmas, I was losing its meaning. But Al knew the real spirit of Christmas when he saw it.

My Three Tenors

December 20, 1995

Three years ago I bought a gift for myself, which opened up a new world of music to me. I ordered the cassette, "Carreras Domingo Pavarotti in concert MEHTA," from my neighbor's daughter through a school fundraiser.

These three gentlemen have been my constant travel companions since. The word is out in my family—wherever Mom goes, so do her three tenors.

My personal benefit of these musicians reaches far beyond pleasure. Unaware of my existence, they have become a strong source of inspiration by virtue of their gifts. The combined result of their voices and the powerful orchestral arrangements strums the chords of my heart and soul.

When I become past the point of feeling, the pathos and passion of their pure tones revive me. When Placido Domingo sings, "*Eluccevan le stelle,*" the musical message transcends the foreign words to identify with my human suffering, lifting me to a level of sweet appreciation for the grief.

Without fail, the mastery of Luciano Pavarotti swells my being with praise and adoration as he sings, "*nessun dorma.*" Indifference passes through the lens of the pure scale, becoming focused affection, making sacrificial love desirable and worthy of the cost. Just like the appeal of precious perfume, the melody has a fragrance that draws me to the one I love.

Most importantly, my three tenors inspired me to dream. The dream became a quest to sing my voice of inspiration to those who are discouraged.

Their songs of emancipation awakened the slumbering artist within me. At first, I believed I was too common to be an artist. Sometimes dreaming is more comfortable than waking to reality.

It's peculiar how an obscure, inexpensive purchase enriched my life exceedingly above its marketed purpose. But I'm not surprised. For the ultimate, most excellent gift—Jesus—came quietly two thousand years ago as a sacrifice for mankind. History records His gift of reconciliation was overlooked by the majority.

But the angels sang their little hearts out, announcing the gift. I just love those angels! They sang the message of the Gift to ordinary shepherds. Music opened their ears and hearts to hear. I believe those shepherds were not the same after that angelic visitation! The story goes they made a bee-line to a manger to visit with the Giver of every good and perfect gift.

I'm so glad my three angels sing to me whenever I want them to. They speak my language. Sweet music. Powerful music. Music that makes me dream and makes my dreams come true. And isn't that a wonderful gift?

Gardens

I carried the bucket of bulbs, shovel and bulb food to the island in my front yard that is my English perennial garden. Fall's agreeable days slipped by, leaving me racing to beat the sleet on a cold November day.

The soil was workable, with the shovel's blade crunching through the frosty surface. The still, crisp air was invigorating. I imagined the new colorful addition of early blooming tulips, irises and daffodils in the spring. With every bulb I planted, my anticipation and appreciation for the spring season grew.

As I was kneeling, digging in the earth, my thoughts wandered to my eldest daughter. She wasn't home last spring, summer, or fall to see the blooms of my garden. How I regretted it! What beauty she missed! I wept at the loss.

Again, I rehearsed the same questions a mother asks when a child she has nurtured decides to trade the shelter of a loving home for the brutality of substance abuse. Again, I answered with the possibilities. The path of this journey is well worn from six years of her coming and going.

The next day, I would be bringing her home from a drug treatment center after a three-year departure from us. Relief refreshed my hope, but reality and experience whispered to me.

Will she be here when my tulips bloom? Will she stay and face each day of winter until spring's visit? Does she know the earth holds the seed of the flower? Will she stay close to the heart of home where love can feed her and restore her soul?

Our prodigal's Christmas card has not been opened. Neither have her Christmas gifts. She left again, leaving behind more heartache, grief and unanswered questions.

The lies she has believed have hardened her heart and devoured her flower.

Friends of a prodigal son encouraged me: "You've done all you can do. There is nothing you can do about her choices. You are not responsible for them. She's in God's hands."

Yes, how painfully I know. With intense desperation I cry out, "I can't pull the weeds that choke the life from her! This child whom I've planted and watered and protected in my life's garden is no longer mine to care for!"

I can't pull the weeds of alcohol and drugs from her earth. How I wish I had the power to stop the violent reaping of addiction! But she must work her own garden. This is the bittersweet place of rest and resignation. It is time to cease from designing, tilling, mulching, planting, transplanting, weeding, fertilizing and watering my garden. I must submit to the frozen ground and wait for the warm sun to thaw the soil and draw forth the flower.

Yes, the seed and bulbs are hidden in the earth. I rest in the reality they will bloom and bear bountiful bouquets again.

Surrendering to the Master Gardener and His seasons is the only hope of peace. With great passion I trust Him with her life. He can cause her garden to bloom again.

Sparking My Memory

January 10, 1996

Poor Sparky. He lay on the ground, shivering with his paws tightly curled under his graying blond body. He looked up at my car, sniffing with his crooked, brown nose, hoping I was one of his family to take him out of the bitter cold. I felt such pity for the dog, wishing I could take him home with me.

This devoted pet waits patiently everyday for his masters, regardless of the weather, on the northeast intersection (hopefully sunny for his warmth) of Townsend and Brewer roads. The first vehicle he recognizes arouses him from the ground, to bound waggingly in excitement.

Sparky has become a neighborhood pet. He joins joggers on their run, and casual walkers on their stroll, sometimes following them home.

My neighbor, Peg, told me her three little girls wanted to adopt Sparky. That's how fondly ol' Sparky is considered around these parts.

But Scott, Sparky's main master, wouldn't hear of it. Everyone knows how crazy Scott is about his dog. A few years ago, Sparky cut his nose badly and Scott panicked. My daughter, Ruth, was present to help Scott with the crisis.

Sparky grew up with Scott. I can't imagine Scott without Sparky. It's been tough enough on both of them since Scott went away to college.

Sweetie, a curly, reddish blond cocker spaniel, was my canine companion during my senior high-school days. We would escape the crowded confusion of a large family, and find a plush grassy spot to lay down and sky-gaze. Sweetie was my pillow as we drank in the quiet of our mutual affection. I would stroke her curly hair as I meditated upon the majestic and mundane. Her loving, brown, puppy dog eyes distracted my thoughts from peer pressure and other worries of life. She listened when I needed to pour out my heart.

It wasn't until after Sweetie's death that I realized how she strengthened my character. She was a haven and a sanctuary for me in times of trouble—a safety valve.

Sweetie was the first beloved creature in my life to die. I grieved her loss amidst of the demands of caring for my small children. I refused to replace her with another dog, protecting myself from the responsibilities of a pet and its inevitable death.

Certainly, it would be impossible to replace Sweetie or Sparky. I thought our almost worthless cat, P. J., might possess Sweetie's qualities since we rescued him from death by bottle-feeding him. Wrong! He keeps the house miceless, but does not appreciate a good quiet time of bonding and sky-gazing.

Twenty years later, I'm wondering if I've protected or deprived myself. Have I prevented all the enjoyment that a dog brings to a family? Did my daughters have a star-gazing companion? I'll have to ask them.

One thing for sure, I'm going to do some serious thinking about this matter. Perhaps I might seek and find a friend like my Sweetie. Until then, Sparky's welcome to drop by for a warm hug anytime.

Dr. Kelly

January 17, 1996

Kelly, my middle daughter, called from Alma College last Thursday night. She wanted to know how I liked my new class at Oakland Community College. Then she asked about her younger sister, Ruth, and her new college classes. The winter semester had begun, and Kelly was checking in on us.

When she is away from home, the sound of her little voice in the phone's handset is music to my ears. There's no greater assurance of her safety than to hear her cheerful, "Hi Mom!"

Kelly possesses one of those compliant, responsible temperaments. Like George Bailey of the movie classic, *It's a Wonderful Life*, she was born old. She never required any serious concern or discipline, developing maturity beyond her years.

Actually, her self-discipline frustrated me during her high-school days. She would close herself in her room, studying for hours to achieve her academic scholarships that made her private college education possible.

I would use cups of hot tea and chocolate to pry some conversation out of her. I needed to hear her say she was doing fine, then I could go on my way. Sometimes she would agree to a fifteen-minute break, devoted to us alone.

A very full life of sports, plays, church and friends left meager remnants of time for Mom. From the moment her dad cut her umbilical chord in the delivery room, our separation began. If I didn't cooperate with life's cycle, there would be certain conflict.

I found myself in the middle of a crossroad. One road read "Hold" and the other "Release." Wisdom told me to prepare myself for her empty room. I had to accept she was going away to college because it was the best choice for her. So, I let her go, with my blessings.

She returns those blessings to me weekly with her phone calls. Last semester, during a conversation, she asked how I was enjoying my French and political science classes. I complained I was drowning in French vocabulary and verb conjugations. And I was anxious about a test.

She counseled, "I used to worry about the same thing, Mom, and you know what? I always did better than what I thought I would. Just relax and do your best. Don't beat your brains out like I did. It's not worth it. There's more to life than a 4.0."

Her words echoed in my mind as I placed the handset down. Listening carefully, the quiet reciprocation of concern calmed my mind. The life cycle was active, bringing transition to our roles. I smiled to myself as I recognized the law of reciprocity in action.

I took Kelly's advice. She was right. My final grades were much better than I expected.

I look forward to Kelly's house calls. Just like a dose of good medicine, they make me feel better.

Childlike

January 31, 1996

My nine-year-old sister, Patty, will celebrate her fortieth birthday on February fifth. Yes, you read correctly. Indulge me please, as I explain.

Patty is the fourth of five daughters. She had her cherubic little legs walking at eight months, dripping her drool behind her. The evidence is forever captured on Dad's home movies, proving her performance. That particular historic film footage draws more *oohs* and *ahhhs* than all the hours Dad filmed.

In retrospect, her first steps were her debut into the entertainment business. She has kept the family laughing with her natural humor and genuine naïveté. Perhaps performing was her means of survival in a family of four daughters. She had central stage until the fifth daughter was born five years later.

Mom and Dad divorced several years before Patty graduated from high school. Life at home wasn't as funny anymore, so her peers became her audience.

But the path of life was kind and Patty returned to the stage of our family once she had her children. The past twenty-five years are marked with crazy and hilarious memories our children produced for us. They were our links between our differences. Patty and I are opposites in many ways, but our mutual appreciation has maintained our relationship.

We made every opportunity of long-distance phone calls and visits to give details of the funny things our kids would do and say. We would work ourselves into tears, laughing at absolutely ridiculous subject matter. I guess Patty was teaching me a healthy form of survival: regression. We developed the ability to regress thirty to forty years in sixty seconds. I'd like to see Mario Andretti break that speed! And a car ride with Patty is more fun than the Gemini at Cedar Point!

A few months ago, Patty told me their latest "family funny." It went like this: The kitchen cabinet above the stove had fallen down. She did her best to rehang it, but it fell down again. A friend told her there was an instrument to locate the studs, so the cabinet would be securely hung by mounting it on the studs instead of the drywall.

She decided to try it. As she was leaving the house for the store to buy this tool that would solve her problems, one of her sons asked, "Mom, where are you going?"

Patty replied, "I'm going to Lowe's to buy a stud-finder."

Her son dryly countered, "Does Dad know about that?"

I laughed as I mentally pictured this scene. Patty's three sons have created a world I would have never known because of my world of four sisters and three daughters. Once again, she dropped another jewel on the scales of my life, balancing the painful with the playful.

It's strange. The most curious metamorphosis has occurred. I'm becoming more like Patty, and she's becoming more like me, yet we have never been more distinctively ourselves. We are mature, yet we have never been more childlike.

Patty takes me places only a child can go. We take little trips away from adult responsibilities and find the kingdom of joy and laughter, where you must be nine years old to enter.

The Write Time

February 7, 1996

The fall Ruth started kindergarten I opened my green note-book, dated the top line, and began a fresh relationship with writing. No more procrastination! The time had arrived. I could not resist the tug of inspiration that flowed from the pages of the book, *Christy*.

Catherine Marshall wrote the novel based on her mother's personal chronicles as a young teacher in the mountains of Tennessee. My Southern heritage related to her story.

Overcoming the feeling of insignificance, I took courage to write. Before the pen touched the paper, I had determined to use prayer as my writing form. I hoped written dialogues with God would develop much needed discipline and structure in my prayer life.

I felt a bit awkward initially, but soon became comfortable with the honesty I could share with the One who knows me best.

The simple tools of paper and pen have mapped my journey of discovery. I soon learned not to condemn myself for failing to write daily. Weekly entries appear in my earlier journals. I forgave myself and picked up where I left off. The paper always listened when I returned.

Inexperience in those early years left gaps where I withdrew in seasons of transition and confusion. Fear of my hidden self prevented me from writing the truth and facing it on the page. But I had to write to see myself. I discovered that writing was the mirror of my soul. Furthermore, if I write honestly about my relationship with God and others, I'll find health.

Once I realized healing by honest confession, I purged myself of secret anger, hatred and fear. My journal was and is a safe dumping ground, sparing my family from much of my personal junk.

The more my conscious self is in agreement with my unconscious self, the less I experience emotional and spiritual conflict and shut-downs. Confusion is avoided by seeing and feeling acutely and accurately.

The pages following the agony of self-realization are filled with thankfulness. Healing brought newfound hope and personal growth. I logged answers to questions and prayers. With anger defused, relationships began to improve. Intimacy was recovered and enhanced. I realized writing expressed my spirit and personality. It is who I am.

Being a gauge of growth, writing also reveals areas where I become stuck. Once I deal with the humiliation of my faults, I can use the energy in being stuck for actually getting somewhere, or helping someone else get somewhere. This requires the most effort of all my writing. I must refuse to stay in those stuck places, leave them behind and proceed to higher ground. Forgive myself and others and continue my journey.

I find my High Tower when I write. Even though my eyesight is fading, I'm seeing things I've overlooked for years. I'm reaching my goal of writing daily because I'm seeing its value. This is the human need to leave my legacy.

Dear reader, I encourage you to record your journey. Befriend your self. This is the write time to begin your story.

Fitting in Love

February 28, 1996

A year ago my very Irish father, Warren O'Brien, was dying of complications due to a surgical heart procedure. A lifetime of smoking and alcohol abuse had destroyed his vascular system. My sisters and I watched his health deteriorate within a year.

Dad's alcoholism had separated him from his family. Year after year, my sisters and I would face the cruel choice of withholding his invitation to family functions and suffering guilt, or inviting him and suffering his obnoxious and hurtful behavior.

My dad was a man who longed to love and express it, but could not overcome his inner weaknesses to do so. My family and I tried every angle to approach our dad, but he never understood the language of love.

We dreaded the day when we would deal with his failing health and death. But not until he was stripped of his strength could he speak those words of love. From February 24 until he died on March 3, 1995, we made every effort to fit in a lifetime of love and forgiveness in those fleeting moments by his bedside.

The following is an entry in my journal that soothes my heart when I remember the life of my lonely father:

"How fitting—I am in Dad's mobile home two weeks exactly after the day he died. Two weeks—two weeks ago I joined my family at my father's deathbed. We became honored guests of a sacred moment in this man's life.

"How thankfulness grows daily for that divine appointment given me and my family! I had never partaken in this deep form of sorrow before I stood at my dad's side. No amount of preparation in dialogue or thought could have softened the impact of watching my father's life leave his body. Even prayer could not ease the wrenching sobs coming from someplace within me. I am unskilled to describe that physical feeling.

"Death was rapidly taking my father. There was nothing we could do. My sisters—thank God for them! We were hoping Dad would live until Sonia arrived, but he hastened to leave us.

"Was he prepared? Could we let him go? That was out of our control. Dad's course was set. His breathing was slowing. He made no response to our cries. The futility of holding him back glared at me without compassion.

"My dad was dying. I sensed the conflict between the assurance of his eternal rest and the need to hear him say once more, 'I love you.' How desperately I needed to hear those words!

"Ranking above that need was the one to express my love to Dad. He was the departing soul and spirit never to return. Ours were the words that needed to be spoken. And we did, with constant affirmations of our love for him and appreciation for the life he had given us.

"Yes, these two weeks have brought many occasions of regret for the years that passed without an exchange of love words. Yes, I do remember his final days when love words were generously shared.

"These two weeks will become two months, then two years, then two decades, then two generations. The love words will become stronger as the weeks become longer.

"How fitting—today is St. Patrick's Day. I wonder if Dad knew the history of his favorite holiday. This shamrock celebration certainly has a new meaning for me. It is the two-week anniversary of my father's death.

"All those frustrated years of blocked love will be overwhelmed in the celebration of Dad's memory. Love's pure embrace is comforting me today. My dad is enjoying the presence of his Creator—the One who designed his shamrock and four-leaf clover."

Now, isn't that fitting?

Emily's Kind of Friend

March 6, 1996

The poet Emily Dickinson expressed her understanding of friendship when she penned, "Long years apart can make no breach a second cannot fill."

Blessed with great riches is a person who shares their life with such a friend. Truly, I pity the individual who cannot be fully human to embrace the depth of emotion provided by a reciprocal relationship. Life is cruel with loneliness, and at the very best bland, without faithful companionship.

Twenty years ago I met an Emily Dickinson type comrade at church. Our young children brought a bond of common interests and concerns. She offered me support during the trying days of childhood disease and development.

I regret I did not preserve a note of encouragement she wrote me when my youngest daughter was hospitalized at four months old. Her graceful handwriting and loving message penetrated my fear and fatigue to refresh my faith. I felt the strength of her love, and knew she was standing by my side.

We shared the following ten years of our lives crying, laughing, dreaming and growing up with our kids. She seemed to be much better at being a friend than I am. She was so sensible, considerate and encouraging. I wanted so much to be more like her. But, she seemed to accept her short end of the friend-stick with great tolerance.

Our lives eventually led us in different directions. My family moved further north, adding distance to the paths between us. Months passed between our rendezvous. We were careful, however, to maintain our connections, talking for hours as we picked up where we left off.

The past and present blended easily, joining our hearts as before.

My friend's birthday is a week before mine in February. She always remembers my birthday with an exceptional card, and I seldom remember hers. I forgot to mail her card this year, and she predictably mailed mine.

I was genuinely disappointed in myself. My friend deserved my thoughtfulness. It was high time to reciprocate.

I sat down and wrote her an apology, asking forgiveness. Belated birthday greetings were included in the card, with copies of various essays of "Encouraging Words."

She called in response to my card and "Encouraging Words." She wept at the discovery of our daughter's struggle with substance abuse. It was time for a reunion with our husbands.

When she greeted us at the door of their home, the months between us vanished. Seated at her dining room table, we covered ground like busy ants, dealing with detail carefully. I left her home fully satisfied in our friendship.

I imagine Emily Dickinson had a friend like my friend, Barb, who taught her how to stand in the gaps of time for a friend. Barb knows the secret place of friendship where a second is as a year, and a year is as a second. In this place, love dwells so richly, time is powerless over matters of the heart.

There is no breach a second of my Barb's love cannot fill.

The Rescuer

March 13, 1996

As children, we all suffer embarrassing experiences that cause great shame. No one is exempt from the demoralizing feeling of exposure, wishing we could disappear or run away and hide.

Years ago, I was one of four judges hired to officiate a gymnastic meet. The little girls, ages eight and nine, looked so darling in their leotards. Those were the days of gymnastic craze, thanks to Mary Lou Retton. The gymnasts giggled as they stretched, tumbled and nervously waited for their turn to compete.

I had judged the floor exercise event for some time when a red headed girl in a light blue leotard stood ready to present herself to the superior judge and me.

Just seconds before the music began for the routine, I noticed the gymnast appearing most distressed. I attempted to make eye contact with the superior judge without success. When I turned to the gymnast, I saw streams of urine running down her legs as she obviously attempted to control her bladder and composure.

It was too late. The music had begun. To my amazement, she began her floor exercise as the trail of wet footsteps marked her humiliation.

I felt so frustrated! I wanted to pull rank and intervene, but it was out of my authority to stop the routine. Couldn't the superior judge see what was happening?

It was impossible to concentrate on scoring her performance. With every step, she danced into shame and tears. How my heart ached for her as I pleaded inwardly for the music to stop. I imagined how her little body trembled inside her thin, wet leotard.

Finally, the music ended. She ran off the mat and into the arms of a tall rescuer who swept her up eagerly. The man held her tightly, as she wrapped her stinging, wet legs around his torso. She found a hiding place in his shoulder, as he held her head close to his. He removed her from the crowded area and disappeared.

I was relieved for the child and grateful for her savior. I hoped he was her father, because that's what fathers are for. A father is his daughter's hero. He is strong enough to lift her above shame into a safe place. He is her defender. He knows when she is hurting and will be there to restore her security.

The scene of the red headed gymnast and the burly, gentle man demonstrates a child's need for a rescuer in times of humiliation. It is a picture of our Father's love for us. I heard a story over forty years ago in Sunday school about a lonely shepherd boy who found his Rescuer. His father rejected him, and didn't see his potential to be a king. But his God did.

I clung to this story as a child, and do now as a parent. Surely, it is impossible for parents to be ever-present protectors of their children. My parents failed me at times, and my husband and I fail our daughters.

How assuring it is to know our Father God will take them up! His arms are always open. They can run to Him and wrap their shame around Him. Disgrace cannot touch them when they hide themselves in Him.

Mirrors

March 20, 1996

Being skin and bones as a child during an age when Shirley Temple was cute, meant to me I was not. Home movies of buck teeth and knobby knees brought laughter which convinced me I was ugly and should avoid cameras and any form of reflection of my thin frame.

I dreamed about being pretty, and filling out the darts in my shirtwaist blouses. But it didn't happen. I would have settled for average looks and a hundred pounds by ninth grade. But it didn't happen. The reflection in the mirror would not change.

Athletics built some muscle, and I finally broke a hundred pounds in high school. And Mom, bless her heart, paid for my orthodontics in my senior year. Her financial sacrifice brought a healthier self-image as I saw improvement in my facial profile.

But insecurities don't die easily. One word can tear down what many have built, especially when the heart is unstable. Eleanor Roosevelt must have spoken from experience when she proclaimed, "No one can make you feel inferior unless you let them." Why do we allow perceptions of others to determine how we see ourselves?

Finding our true beauty can be a life-long journey. If we are looking for a mere image, our soul will never be satisfied with what we see. Isn't this the hunger of every human being? To be accepted for our selves and not our shells?

I asked this question at a journal workshop I recently presented. After teaching and encouraging a group of women to abandon their self-image and write their innermost thoughts, I gave them time for writing practice. They were given opportunity to share their entries. With each word they read, parts of their outer selves peeled away, revealing the diamond of their soul.

Peggy glowed with understanding as she read her journal entry. She is a widow and grandmother of teenagers. She read her written words with great emotion, warning those present she might not make it to the end. Her real self rose from her heart, passed through her throat and surfaced in tears.

Peggy related an experience of that morning. She stood in front of the bathroom mirror, preparing for the workshop, and worshipping God in the process. When she looked at her face in the mirror, she saw herself differently. There was a beauty that went deeper than her face. The insecurities that pulled her down to doubt were lost in the awareness of who she is.

Peggy stepped beyond the boundaries of self-consciousness and explored the crystalline stream that flows from the reservoir of everything she is from the time she was. When she wrote about the mirror, she used the first thought as the creative force to tap the unconscious riches of her true identity.

Those of us present saw the real Peggy, not an image of her self. Our unconscious selves related to hers, therefore, establishing a purer relationship with her. We witnessed how reflections can only provoke the rational but identification accomplishes the relational.

Peggy encouraged us by her trust and transparency. We benefited by her willingness to risk honesty. Her wonderful words of life stabilized the houses of our character. Peggy proved to me once again this truth: When we are real—transparent—we find our essence of beauty. This is being who we were created to be. *Being* beautiful changes our reflection in our mirrors.

I don't run from mirrors anymore, for they only reflect my image and not the real me. When I'm tempted to be afraid of human mirrors, I remind myself they may not reflect who I am. My shell is not my identity. And my identity cannot be reflected because it is transparent.

Living Legacy

April 3, 1996

My head throbbed with a migraine headache as I climbed the dark-stained steps of Victor Hugo's home in Paris. The pictures hanging on the stairway walls were fascinating, regardless of the pain to focus my eyes on their detail.

I heard children's playful voices as I approached a window on the landing. The tiny opening revealed a court-yard, busy with the revelry of recess. I lingered, leaning closer to the open window for a wider view, amused with the sights, sounds and smells of the May day.

I was realizing a dream. Victor Hugo introduced me to France as a high-school sophomore through his novel, *Les Misérables*, and the story has lived in me since.

I left the window and continued the tour. Having seen the musical three times and listened for countless hours to the CD, my mind was alive with references to the characters Victor Hugo created.

Then I found what I was looking for: his famous drawing of the young girl, Cosette, which symbolizes his story all over the world. The art expresses the haunting depravation of the abandoned child before ransomed by Jean Valjean, the main character of the story.

Just recently, Victor Hugo touched me again through the PBS tenth-anniversary presentation of the stage play, *Les Misérables*. The performances were superb, as each character uncovered messages I had previously missed.

The play has a living relationship with human suffering. The theme of the story has no boundaries to culture or time, for mankind is ever in the need of redemption from oppression.

Jean Valjean is released from 17 years of prison for stealing a loaf of bread to feed a starving relative. But the heart of the message is found in the relentless Javert, the officer assigned to Valjean, who doesn't understand forgiveness and the changing power of grace. Because Javert is bound by the law of judgment, he rejects Valjean's conversion, and believes with all his strength that Valjean must suffer for his crime.

Javert's mission is to execute judgment upon Valjean. Valjean flees from Javert to fulfill his promise to care for Cosette until she is grown. When the tables turn and Javert is discovered as a spy against the young leaders at the student barricade, Valjean pretends to kill him, insisting Javert escape.

Javert finds his world falling in on him. Valjean's compassion and integrity grants Javert freedom that causes him to doubt all he is and all he believes. With fisted heart, he closes himself to redemption, becoming a prisoner of unbelief. He sees no escape from the world of Jean Valjean, so he plunges to his death in the Seine River.

Valjean lived to see his darling Cosette securely married to the man she loved. He endured suffering to see his reward. He found peace and rest at the end of his journey.

For an encore of the PBS presentation, seventeen actors who played Valjean's role sang the finale. They represented the seven continents where the play was performed. A mammoth print of Cosette was raised on stage as red, white and blue balloons were released throughout the theater.

I also celebrated as I marveled how Victor Hugo's message of redemption has traveled the world. His legacy lives and grows through his gifts. They encourage me to hold my hand open—open to give and receive grace in times of suffering. As Valjean discovered, the candle of grace will light my path to freedom.

And that candle shines upon young Cosette's eyes—eyes that represent the oppressed. Will I execute judgment or will I join the crusade to find the place where children play?

Blueberry Pancakes

April 17, 1996

Denny loves his three sons with rare devotion. Our children grew up together, giving me opportunities to see his paternal feelings push through his tough exterior and leak through his eyes.

One of Denny's favorite ways to express his love for his boys was to take them downhill skiing. The four of them would tear up the slopes, racing, jumping and having the time of their lives. I've seen them in action. Very impressive. Their annual ski trips were probably anticipated with greater enthusiasm than Christmas. I say *were* because his two older sons are now married, and the youngest, Mike, is a senior in high school. The guys don't take many ski trips together since the grandchildren arrived.

The last time we were together, Denny mentioned he kept a journal of several ski trips. I persuaded him to share it with me. As Denny scanned the journal, he found the entry where Mike had promised to make blueberry pancakes for breakfast. When the guys attempted to wake him up in the morning to make him keep his word, he snapped, "Shut up and get outta here." The next line read, "So we had toast and corn flakes."

We laughed and continued reading until we found the footnote of the next day, "Oh yeah, believe it or not, Mike got up and made blueberry pancakes in the morning." Denny's eyes twinkled inimitably, revealing the pleasure he remembered.

Those blueberry pancakes meant a lot to Denny. Perhaps the way to a man's heart is through his stomach. But if I know Denny, Mike fed more than his dad's stomach. Mike fed their relationship. Sure, Denny enjoys blueberry pancakes, but I believe he was asking for something else. He was asking Mike for his friendship, for involvement in his life. He was asking, Are you enjoying our time together? Do you value our relationship? Are you willing to put something back into it?

Parents search for evidence of responsibility, respect and growth in their children. The simplest considerations please a parent and prove they are appreciated. There's something about sitting down at a table and bragging about the meal your boy made. It's bonding. Communion. Communication.

Mike probably has no clue how much he satisfied his father with his blueberry pancakes. That's okay. Someday he'll be on the other side of the parent–child table. If life takes its usual turns, he'll be silently asking those same questions of his children.

Hopefully he will remember the toast and corn flakes and his father's waiting eyes. He'll remember the sound of snow cutting under the skis. The scene of jumps over moguls and races downhill will flash in his mind.

All this excitement will make him very hungry. Then the aroma of biueberry pancakes will leak into his mind.

He'll smile and remember it's the simple expressions of love that nurture the human spirit.

Memory Makers

May 8, 1996

I was feeling a bit blue as I removed the plastic bubble wrapping from the Easter ceramics. Each bunny, duck and chick reminded me of my daughters' childhood days.

A fleeting thought dared suggest I not bother with my traditional Easter decorating this year. Self pity and loneliness lied, "No one will even notice. You're the only one who really cares about these silly things, anyway."

"I'm doing this for myself!" I rebuked. Continuing my self-talk, I climbed the basement stairs with my arms full of ceramic memories. My artistic mother-in-law lovingly made each Easter memento. During their precious young years, my girls would find a package delivered by UPS just before Easter. They would tear it open to find another personalized item from Grandma Rosie, stuffed with mouthwatering Fanny Farmer chocolate.

As I cleaned the clay critters and arranged green straw and colored plastic eggs around them, my nesting instincts brought a sense of rightness to my soul. I felt completely comfortable with where I was and what I was doing. I was in my place—even if it was an empty nest.

Pausing in reflection, my mind's eye could see my three darlings, dressed in their home-sewn Easter dresses and coats, chasing around the house to find their Easter baskets. Nostalgia served me memories of my mother and the Easter outfits she sewed for her five daughters.

Mom was a sewing machine slave, and loved her bondage. I would wager a bet she spent more time feeding the needle of the sewing machine than she did her family! I can still hear the hum coming from the kitchen where she created garments for her girls.

There was security in seeing her leaning into the light of the machine, burning the midnight oil. As a child, the security was an unconscious feeling that developed my character. As an adult, I see clearly the role of Mom's sewing machine in my life.

Listening in the sunlight of the dining room, the silent Easter animals told me how important they are to my children. I understood again the mystery of motherhood and the awkward empty nest.

Mothers are memory-makers. Their role never changes. They make unconscious deposits into the memory banks of their children until the day they die. Just at the right time, children withdraw these riches when they need them, until the day they die.

Memories only gain interest in the vault of the human heart. Their dividends are beyond an expert's ability to calculate. Memories live forever in their mysterious places, waiting to fill the wanting places of the soul.

When my vacant, hollow house tempts me with loneliness, I'll force my mind to think upon the two most important women in my life who are the most excellent memory makers. They successfully cut the apron strings from their children, and I will too.

Mothers instinctively shift their creative energies from their children to their grandchildren. In my present barren place, memories are my companions of truth when deception tries to lure me from my calling as a mother.

I don't quite know what to do with myself without children around. But one thing is certain. I will continue to make memories and honor traditions because the womb of a mother's heart is always fertile, ever conceiving and delivering simple and profound experiences that develop into memories.

My mothers have given me courage to remain in my place. They visit me in my melancholy and remind me traditions and memory-making are worth the effort.

They tell me my children really do care about bunnies, ducks and chicks. They just don't know it. But they will— when they are moms.

Delicious

May 15, 1996

A sunbeam squeezed between the drawn shade and frame of my bedroom window and told me to get up and attend to my flowerbeds.

Finally, spring had arrived. How I anticipated this day every year! Michigan's enduring winters create a cause for celebration for the first warm, sunny day. This was a particularly premium Saturday—just a slight breeze to refresh the face with spring's delicious scents.

My husband and I worked furiously to prepare spring to shed forth her glory through our hand-me-down lilac bushes, peonies, tulips, lilies of the valley, irises and trillium. We uncovered our "little Ireland" as we removed the dead remnants of scrappy brown grass and plants. Oh, how I love green!

As I labored in the sun, a taste for ice cream rolled over my tongue and would not leave. At day's end, I twisted Mel's arm to drive us into the Ice Cream Saloon in Romeo to satisfy this desire. After all, there had to be some reward for this middle-aged aching body!

The screen door revealed the crowded curiosity of Michiganders who were probably enjoying their first official ice cream of the season. The excitement was as savory as the smell of waffle cone and chocolate. Children of all sizes leaned against the glass case, drooling over their options.

Only a hot fudge sundae could quench my craving. Mel ordered a cone. My treat was prepared first. My mouth watered as I raced to the tables, staring at the cherry on top of the real whipped cream. I sat down and wriggled inside to dig in. I looked for Mel. I couldn't find him in the crowd, so I plunged the spoon into my temptation, too anxious to wait.

Sweet satisfaction! Not until after the first two bites did I return to consciousness from the "sundae spell."

When I lifted my eyes from my coveted dish, a pair of boyish black eyes were staring at me. Uh oh, wasn't I minding my manners? Did I have chocolate fudge stringing from my chin?

Adding to my embarrassment, I noticed the lad and his companions were waiting patiently for their orders. I made a quick attempt to behave like an adult.

The youth asked, "You're really enjoying that, aren't you?"

I was surprised by his purely spontaneous question, as he related to the child in me. He noticed I was there and he engaged with me. I felt a part of his world and youthfulness. He gave me permission to enjoy my ice cream like a child. And I did (but resisted the urge to lick the dish).

As Mel and I drove home, purples and pinks colored the sky with promises of a repeat performance. I relaxed my weary muscles, leaned back on the headrest, and rolled the taste of the day over my mind.

It had been delicious—from the first friendly ray of sunrise to the assuring farewell of the sunset. And inside my aching bones was one very contented little girl.

Waiting

May 22, 1996

Several months ago, during a sisters' get-away-weekend, one of my sisters spoke words of wisdom on the subject of waiting. She caught my interest because among our family, she has the reputation of being the most impulsive. She spoke honestly of her struggle with impatience and the desire to avoid the suffering required to reach her goals. She confessed she was discovering the value in surrendering to the waiting that life forced upon her.

As she opened this private door of her life, I walked into a new understanding of my sister. I knew of many circumstances that could have destroyed her and her family, had she not waited for the storms of adversity to blow over her household. But her roots were deep in the earth of experience. Strong winds had bent—but not broken—her.

My sister had grown. She was not the same impetuous person she was five years ago. I was impressed and intrigued. It wasn't her words that spoke to me—it was her poise. Her attitude toward waiting had changed. Waiting was no longer her enemy, but her friend. The energy she once used to avoid waiting was transformed to use waiting for her benefit.

Just how did she accomplish this? Practice. She turned her face into the storm and stood. She waited with expectation of its passing. She learned to wait by standing and watching.

Isn't it strange how people don't know how to wait? Whether the situation is tragic or trivial, we are awkward in the waiting cycle of life's experiences. We bail out of the challenge by withdrawal or retaliation.

Traffic is a case in point. Is there a more common waiting-room to the American citizen than their vehicle? Have you ever attempted to explain to your young child what that obscene hand gesture meant, and why the person

45

in the other car was so mad at you? Why do we run red lights? We just don't want to wait. Heaven help anyone who gets in our way! We become violent when we are subjected to waiting.

Waiting in a restaurant is another illustration. Isn't it strange how people are usually more civil in public places than their personal vehicles? I think it's so peculiar how people withdraw and pretend no one else is waiting in line next to them. We don't know how to wait and be friendly.

Mel and I were in the waiting line at Red Knapp's one Friday night. The restaurant is new to Oxford and gathers great crowds from the surrounding area. A young couple with a son and daughter stood next to us. I couldn't help but hear their conversation among themselves. I asked where they called home.

"Lapeer," they answered.

We entertained ourselves with our waiting companions for fifteen minutes. Jimmy, the eight-year-old son, proudly gave details about his principal's delivery of a rose to his teacher the day and moment he announced to Mrs. M. she had been voted the "teacher of the year" in their school district.

Jimmy told Mel and me how Mrs. M. cried when the principal gave her the rose. Then he added, "We cried, too."

"You must really like her," I guessed.

"Oh, yeah," Jimmy emphatically replied, "she's the best teacher, and we love her. Everyone loves her."

Jimmy made waiting enjoyable until "Underwood Party" was called. The attitude of his family made waiting a pleasant experience. Something worth thinking and writing about.

The following are Webster's definitions of "wait": 1) to stay in place in expectation, 2) to delay serving (a meal), 3) to remain stationary in readiness or expectation, 4) to pause for another to catch up, 5) to hold back expectantly, 6) to be ready and available, and 7) a state of attitude or watchfulness and expectancy.

No matter how you read it, "wait" is positive. Jimmy proved even delaying a meal can be enjoyable. The Old English word for "wait" is "watch." Waiting is an active process. By watching we are available to learn something neat about little boys and life in Lapeer.

We build endurance by standing and watching. We develop spiritual muscles to withstand the fierce trials of our patience and faith. Can we pause long enough for a loved one to catch up with us? Just how long do we wait? And how do we wait?

If we didn't have coaches to remind us, "this too shall pass," we would throw in the towel when waiting becomes uncomfortable or painful. We would sacrifice the prize set before us. And we have, plenty of times.

Patty and Jimmy encourage me to stand, watch and wait. They remind me that the bitterest words in life are, "See what you missed?"

No Silly Goose

June 5, 1996

It seems the Underwood house is located beneath a geese flight-route. I have observed countless occasions of crossings above my head, as I curiously inspect the flying, flapping V.

One such crossing was exceptional to all others. I was on my knees, digging in my flowers, when a strange honking sound broke the silent serenity I was enjoying. I spied a multitude of geese as I stood to find the cause of the racket.

There were several large V's going west. I had never heard or seen anything like it before or since. I felt the surge of something similar to inspiration as the volume of the honking increased. Captivated by the mystery of nature, I watched and listened until the geese were out of sight and sound.

I decided to attempt a study of geese and their behavior in hopes to understand their effect upon me. Were these birds telling me something? I was developing an appreciation for and an interest in geese.

My good intentions never took me to the library or bookstore to research the birds. I accidentally found what I was looking for in an office one day at work. The title, "LESSONS FROM GEESE," caught my attention. A Xerox copy of the following was taped on the wall.

FACT 1: As each goose flaps its wings it creates an "uplift" for the birds that follow. By flying in a V formation, the whole flock adds 71% greater flying range than if each bird flew alone.

LESSON: People who share common direction and sense of community can get where they are going quicker and easier because they are traveling on the thrust of one another.

FACT 2: When a goose falls out of formation, it suddenly feels the drag and resistance of flying alone. It quickly moves back into formation to take advantage of the lifting power of the bird immediately in front of it.

LESSON: If we have as much sense as a goose we stay in formation with those headed where we want to go. We are willing to accept their help and give our help to others.

FACT 3: When the lead goose tires, it rotates back into the formation and another goose flies to the point position.

LESSON: It pays to take turns doing the hard tasks and sharing leadership. As with geese, people are interdependent on each other's skills, capabilities and unique arrangements of gifts, talents and resources.

FACT 4: The geese flying in formation honk to encourage those up front to keep up their speed.

LESSON: We need to make sure our honking is encouraging. In groups where there is encouragement, the production is much greater. The power of encouragement (to stand by one's heart or core values and encourage the heart and core of others) is the quality of honking we seek.

FACT 5: When a goose gets sick, wounded or shot down, two geese drop with it until it dies or is able to fly again. Then, they launch out with another formation to catch up with the flock.

LESSON: If we have as much sense as geese, we will stand by each other in difficult times as well as when we are strong.

My mystery is solved. The "something" I felt from the honking geese was the fallout of their encouragement. They were telling me to keep plugging away, pulling up weeds of doubt and planting seeds of faith.

The facts and lessons make sense, just like the geese. I will never call my friendly fowl a "silly goose" again.

(*Note*: "Lessons from Geese" was transcribed from a speech given by Angeles Arrien at the 1991 Organizational Development Network and was based on the work of Milton Olson.)

Little Red Slippers

June 12, 1996

My favorite page of *Southern Living* magazine is the last page, titled "Southern Journal." Every issue provides worthy stories of Southern interest, and if you have a Southern heritage and hankerings, you'll be interested.

A recent issue reminisced a special day in the author's childhood. One of his aunts had taken him, at age nine, to the big city of Montgomery, Alabama, for a day's shopping. It was his first experience in a large department store, with lunch on the mezzanine. He remembered the wooden glider purchased in the toy department. He drank his first cup of coffee (more milk than coffee) sitting on a stool next to his aunt in a little diner.

I identified with the author, for my aunts and uncles added a dimension to my life unique to them. The story "got me to thinkin'" about my young nieces and nephews in Grand Rapids, and how I'm missing so much of their lives. I purposed to take time for them this summer.

My sister soon gave me opportunity to fulfill my desire with the news of their move from Grand Rapids to Dayton, Ohio. I offered to take her kids for several days while she investigated matters in Dayton—but only after selfishly questioning the move.

Kirk stayed at home with Dad and went to school. Erin, Victoria and Kaci visited for three days. What fun!

Kelly (my daughter who happened to be home for semester break) danced with the three girls to Beethoven's Ninth Symphony. Erin, the nine-year-old, didn't know if she appreciated music. Victoria and Kaci are too young to make any judgments. They just giggled and danced. I left the kitchen long enough to join the fun. They laughed louder as I leaped to "Ode to Joy."

Victoria, the four-year-old, whirled around in her little red slippers. Little slippers have a soft spot in my heart. My girls had pink terry slippers for their dancing.

Kelly and I exhausted ourselves having fun with and taking care of the three girls. Erin and Kaci joined me for grocery shopping while Victoria stayed home with Kelly and danced.

We went to see the movie, *James and the Giant Peach*, which provoked endless questions from Victoria, which provoked Erin. She coached me how to ignore Victoria to put an end to her questions. *The Velveteen Rabbit* put the girls to bed. Thankfully, Victoria was too busy eating popcorn to ask many questions.

They all settled in Kelly's room (the all-purpose room) for their last night's sleep at Aunt Iris's house.

I reclined in my chair with hot tea, ready to rest, read and write. I wanted to capture on paper the goodnight hugs and kisses, and the feeling I felt watching Kaci fall asleep next to me.

Kelly, obviously over-worked, asked, "Mom, why do you have company every time I come home? It sure would be nice to have my own bed to sleep in every once in a while."

"I know, Kell, but your room is the most practical for guests. It's easier to shift you around than three persons. You know, my sister is moving soon, and we may not have an opportunity like this for a long time. I can't help it, Kell. My mom gave me the gift of hospitality."

Kelly listened to my reasoning, then climbed the stairs to share her sister's bed. She returned after several minutes to apologize. "I'm sorry for being so selfish, Mom."

I stood and hugged her with thanks for all her help with the girls. We both headed for bed, passing Victoria's little red slippers that were side-by-side on the floor. Kelly paused to point to the floor. "Look, Mom. Victoria's slippers."

We towered in admiration over the red, satin slippers with a tiny cluster of pearls on top. "They look like they're waiting for her, don't they? Kell, I would not have missed this for the world." She smiled in agreement.

My heart danced like Victoria's slippers. I was thankful Kelly had ears to hear. I was thankful she had eyes to see.

She saw something that made that day special in the life of a middle-aged aunt. Little red slippers.

Turkey Toes

June 26, 1996

Do you take life and yourself too seriously? Can you laugh at yourself when caught in a potentially embarrassing situation, or do you become tense and self-conscious?

Thank goodness, I've lived long enough to see my critics are correct—I need to learn to laugh at myself. I guess that's one advantage to aging. Eventually, we realize our faults and accept them. We wear out and relax our control, easing efforts to perform perfectly for people and ourselves. We arrive at the deep, philosophical question, "What's the big deal, anyway?"

The first weekend in June offered a laughably enlightening experience for about seven thousand women and me. We listened to four women speak about their journey from the pits of despair to the peaks of joy—using the healing gifts of joy and laughter. The audience roared until some of us cried.

My small group of "gals" checked into a hotel near the seminar location Friday night; Jan, Libby and Kathy in one room, Mary and I in another. We met at a local Mickey D's for our brief, budget breakfast Saturday morning. Being a bit giddy from the lack of sleep and the simple fact we were away from our kids and husbands, we were primed to laugh at anything remotely funny.

While we were eating and chatting, someone complimented Kathy on the "sweet" dress she was wearing. The dress indeed accentuated her natural beauty.

In response, Kathy swung her legs from under the table and looked down at her feet. "Thank you. And look, my shoes match my dress." She wiggled her feet around to model her sandals.

We were all admiring the match when Kathy baited, "How do you like my turkey toes?"

Laughter erupted from Kathy, Jan and Libby, while Mary and I sat in the dark to this inside joke. Naturally, we questioned, "Turkey toes?"

Libby began to clue us in. "Kathy had just made it into the bathroom this morning when I needed to use it. I heard the shower on, but wasn't sure if she was in the shower with the curtain closed, so I knocked on the door and asked her if the curtain was closed because I needed to use the bathroom."

She finished between chuckles, "Kathy thought I asked her if she had turkey toes, and answered, 'Yeah, I have turkey toes.'"

All five of us were cracking up by that point, wondering why in the world would Kathy have answered such a bizarre question.

In defense, Kathy added, "I thought it was strange for Libby to be asking me about my toes, but they are funny looking. It was too early to be thinking clearly, and I couldn't hear her because the shower was on. So I answered, "Yeah, I have turkey toes."

We made good laughing mileage out of Kathy's toes that day. As a matter of fact, every time we think about turkey toes, we laugh. She proved the point of our weekend adventure: a healthy sense of humor permits us to accept the things we cannot change, making inferiority impossible and life a lot more fun.

Deck 10

July 10, 1996

Mel and I met Vince and Tina last year on a cruise of the Greek islands. We enjoyed one of life's first experiences with them, archiving the four of us in our photos until moths and mold corrupt. Among the ruins of Athens, we discovered we had a lot in common. Vince and Mel are in the floor covering business (we were traveling with Mel's company). Tina and I love cappuccino and baklava — especially in an outdoor café at the base of the Acropolis. Life is good.

We rented mopeds and puttered around the Island of Santorini together. A red cliff scrolled above one of the beaches like a tidal wave to provide the perfect backdrop for the perfect picture (and you can bet I snapped one). Blinding white buildings were carved into the sides of the cliffs, making breathtaking views of the Mediterranean where we could enjoy our Greek salad.

Unaware, Vince and Tina were companions in my recovery from near emotional and physical collapse. The demands and damage of our daughter's substance abuse had threatened to break me, with the blows continuing until we departed for the airport.

I was never so thankful and needy for an opportunity to fly away as I was at that point in my life. I felt like the proverbial bird, escaping from the claws of death.

Maybe Vince and Tina sensed my fragile frame of mind. I don't know. They brought life back into perspective, nonetheless. Their gentle and humorous personalities were what any doctor would have ordered. I returned home refreshed.

Just six weeks ago, Mel and I found ourselves on another company Mediterranean cruise with Vince and Tina! (I know what you're thinking: Life is tough!) But this time, our foursome grew to six, adding Ron and Gail, who are good friends and Mel's customers. They hit it off great with Vince and Tina, adding a special touch to our visits to Pompeii, Palma de Mallorca and Barcelona.

We six soaked up the sights, trying not to miss a thing. Then we headed for our three-day extension to Paris. Yes! I love Paris! We ran like American maniacs through the streets of Paris because Ron and Gail were flying home the next morning. Ron shot three rolls of film in six hours. We closed down the Metro at 1 a.m., getting stranded on the Champs Elysees.

The last night in Paris we were down to the foursome from Greece. We toured Luxembourg's Gardens on the most weather-perfect evening in history. We posed for a photo by a miniature Statue of Liberty found on the edge of the Gardens. A little old Frenchman with tobacco-stained fingers used my camera to snap the memory. I thanked him in my Beginning French 1. I was awesome!

We found a French-Italian restaurant to savor our final meal and evening together. Tiramisu and other mouth-watering temptations concluded a three-hour meal on Rue Saint Michael.

Longing to linger, Vince asked what we considered the highlight of our ten-day adventure. We took turns telling. Tina's choice was the day sunning on the ship. Mine were too numerous to name. Mel thought of Barcelona first. Vince said, "I liked deck 10 the best."

"Deck 10?" I probed.

Vince reflected, "Yeah, that's where the coffee was. That's where we ate together and talked … we leaned over the rail and watched the ports come and go together."

Vince got me to thinking. I could see why he and Tina have a way of softening hardships, molding them into positive experiences — they understand and value the intimacy of friendship.

How could we possibly swallow suffering and sorrow without the sweet servings of friendship? Isn't it amazing how we draw quiet strength from holding a cup of hot coffee in the presence of a friend? There is a mysterious exchange in the steam as it circles above the coffee. Our losses are compensated by gains in those hallowed places of friendship.

Could this be why I love Paris? Do I sense the intimacy of companionship in the crowded cafés? Could this be why American youth fall in love with Paris (Europe, in general)? Is this why coffeehouses are springing up all over the U.S.?

Perhaps we are learning that everyone needs to find a friend, and a place where their hearts can meet. Indeed, everyone needs a deck 10.

There Will Always Be a Becky

July 31, 1996

Death is demanding. Grief is unpredictable. I am over-whelmed with both. Winter has blasted my July with this reality: my darling Becky died. With no *good-byes* — no *I love you*. No final embraces.

I wept tears of protest as I salvaged eucalyptus and choice flowers from the dead floral arrangements we received from friends and family. "It's not right I should suffer the agony of gathering the remnants of Becky's life, and now her death. I gave birth to her. I gave her my love. I cherished her with my life! Everything dies. The end of life is too brutal. How can I bear this, Lord?"

An answer came gently, "It is an honor to serve Becky in her death." Understanding eased the injustice of my responsibility. I asked God for the strength to honor Becky in attending to the necessary details of her death. No one else can fill this role. This is my appointment.

As I emptied the vases and baskets into the garbage can, the oldest of the three neighbor girls walked toward me and into the garage. Her sympathetic eyes told me she brought comfort. We embraced. I could feel her body heaving sobs of sorrow. She spoke no words, only held me tight.

I appreciated her silence. Probing questions about the cause of Becky's death have caused me to withdraw from people. But I was safe with this fourteen-year-old. We were safe with each other.

I have no secrets. She knows about Becky's troubles. Her family moved into their new home eight years ago on the same cold February weekend we moved into ours. She witnessed Becky's coming and going from our driveway and our efforts to deal with the painful tide.

Finding only weak words of comfort, I asked her if there was anything she wanted to tell me, or if she had any questions. She nodded a tearful yes. We found a private place in my backyard to sit and share our hearts.

She asked, "What was Becky like?"

I had not anticipated her question. Pausing to gain composure and gather my thoughts, I realized she did not have the pleasure of knowing Becky before she became a prisoner of substance abuse.

For some sweet moments, I reminisced Becky's lively childhood. Her outgoing personality and quick sense of humor. Her athletic abilities that were premiered at a company picnic where she won all the races and medals at age seven. She continued running through high school, winning state championships in cross country and track. She was a competitor.

I spoke of her sensitive spirit. She loved animals. That's why we have our cat, P. J. She brought him home as an abandoned newborn kitten six years ago. We took turns dropper and bottle-feeding him to health. P. J. is a family effort.

She was naturally beautiful and intelligent. Good grades came easily, as well as an active social life. But she kept her feelings locked up inside.

The bitter memories of the lies and deception returned the well-worn questions as I searched for reasons for Becky's departure from the truth and her family. All I could answer my little friend was, "The lies made Becky so confused, and the addictions became too strong for her. She wanted to be the woman she once was, but she couldn't. Perhaps God knew her weaknesses, and took her home to Him. We wanted her well and with us, and it hurts so badly that she chose a different home."

I admonished my friend to trust her parents, and to talk to them even when it is difficult. As we held each other, I whispered, "Becky, promise me you won't believe the lies."

"I promise, Mrs. Underwood."

"I love you, Becky."

"I love you too."

"Your parents love you. Do you believe that?"

"Uh-huh."

I gave her one final squeeze and watched her walk across my yard and into hers. Another Becky had brought me love and forever bonded our hearts. I prayed God would give her strength to keep her promise.

We are surrounded by little women like my Becky and the Becky next door. My mother's heart hopes and prays each one will find someone to embrace and honor their innocence.

The sword of sorrow has pierced my soul. My first-born was torn from my being, leaving an abortive wound. Only the blessed salve of assurance reminds me that Jesus was her best friend, the One who was the Light in her darkness and the Guide to the way of peace.

I know very little of this earth and universe, but I do know my Becky is no longer tormented by lies, but is somewhere wrapped in the arms of eternal truth.

Front Porch Fast Food

August 7, 1996

I balked at the news when my sister, Sonia, first told me they were moving back to Dayton, Ohio. I had so much enjoyed their location in Grand Rapids for the past four years. My in-laws live there also, making a very convenient visiting arrangement for both sides of the family.

Sonia was quick with a firm reprimand for my lack of enthusiasm.

"Iris, I called for your support. I need it right now. This isn't going to be easy for me."

She accepted my apology and efforts to explain my response. We understand my motherly tendencies. Mom brought her home from the hospital when I was nearly thirteen years old. She was the most beautiful baby I had ever seen. With few exceptions (when she mistreated my dog, Sweetie), I have adored her from that day forward.

Sonia developed into an amazing mother of four children. Her husband, Brent, is an equally devoted parent. They are a dynamic duo. I saw them in action during the moving process last week.

Sonia and the kids packed their ten-room home while Brent was learning the ropes at his new job in Dayton. I arrived on Thursday to help with the remaining packing, loading and cleaning. The plan was to stay as long as my energy permitted.

After a good night's rest, I decided to stay another day and night. I phoned Kathy at Kelly Services on Friday to confirm an assignment. She was expecting my call from Grand Rapids, for I had previously informed her of my plans to help my sister move.

During our conversation, Kathy remarked, "It sounds like you have a strong support system."

"Yes, we do. I don't know what we would do without each other." Gratitude grew as Kathy's words echoed in my mind. Yes, I support Sonia, she supports me. There is an invisible system working between us.

She welcomed my broken, grieving heart into her hectic time of transition. We were both offering what we could give at the time: our loving support.

Before they pulled the U-Haul out of the driveway, we ate fast food on the front porch of the house. Brent thanked me for my help, with Sonia and the kids adding their sentiments of appreciation. I told them, "It was my pleasure." And it was.

They were leaving the home of our last Thanksgiving Day with Becky, and the celebration of her last birthday. Now it was a house that belonged to someone else. They gave me the chance to say good-bye. Another sad passage. Another "place" to let go. One of those painful pleasures.

The drive home gave time for tears and meditation. I saw my family as a respirator, breathing life into my languishing lungs.

There were more sympathy cards waiting for me at home. The words of comfort lifted death's pressure from my chest, giving me strength to face the night.

I would never have chosen the receiving end of sympathy. Who would? It is more comfortable to give support than to receive it. But here I am, in a needy place, receiving countless expressions of support.

The abundant goodness evident in people encourages my heart. This grace overwhelms the evil violence of the world, preventing the cynic from moving into my house.

I will stay hooked up to my life-support systems. And I would encourage you to do the same. We all need support right now. Life isn't going to get any easier.

Margie's for a Keepsake

August 14, 1996

I'm so glad I remembered Kristie's birthday. My sister, Linda, chose me as her godmother 26 years ago. I've basically grown up with my niece, not fully appreciating my honored rank until my more mature years.

I invited her to Margie's for breakfast last Saturday. It's one of those places where the Lake Orion local color is the only interior design you will find — and we love it that way. Every little town has a meetin' place like Margie's — if they're worth their weight in salt.

If you're not careful, the old wooden screen door will greet you with a smack in the "be-hind" as you enter the busy hodgepodge of people, who have their face in their grub and don't notice you or the noisy slam.

Kristie waved me over to our booth. Yes! That's my favorite seat, right by the grill where the action is, and all those early morning smells. Reaching my seat, Andrea, Kristie's sister, surprised me with her smile when I discovered her behind the tall seat. Wonderful! The more the merrier!

I sat next to the birthday girl, presenting her with a rose bouquet from my garden and a tiny wrapped and ribboned gift box. Andrea followed her decorating instincts and arranged the splash of pink on our table. *Voilà!* Our down-home dining now had a woman's touch.

I dug my mental spurs into the soil of Margie's earth, returning to the life Robert Frost advocated in his poem, "Directive." Yep, I was home. Cozy. Even the booth fit like a familiar chair.

You don't rush life at Margie's. As Kristie opened her gift, I wished we could slow the moment into a thousand. This was the most special gift I had ever presented her. Could she sense the unspeakable desires of my heart? As she unwrapped the box, I explained the gift was purchased in Marseille, France, during our last Mediterranean cruise. Kristie removed the last layer of tissue to find the miniature heart-shaped porcelain box, with hand-painted flowers on the cover. The girls said it was beautiful.

Emotion changed my voice and tears smarted my eyes as I explained, "It was intended for Becky's heart collection."

"Yeah, I remember seeing Becky's hearts all over the place, and wondering were they came from. Now I know."

I bought a heart-box for Becky years ago during a trip and made a tradition of it. There were only a few times I couldn't find one during my travels.

"I wanted you to have this one. Thank you for being a faithful cousin and friend to Becky." She accepted my gift with a comforting hug. Her arms squeezed 25 years of memories out of my swelling heart. Kristie as a butterfly for Halloween, Becky as the flower. Kristie fluttered around Becky. It was hard for Becky to stand still and let Kristie fly. It's all on film — thank God.

Oh, if only I were a rich woman like Tevye sang (father in *Fiddler on the Roof*), I would whisk my nieces away and take them across the ocean to discover the simple and rich places and people I have enjoyed. I dreamed the same dream for my three daughters.

Now I must alter my dreams to fit two.

And Kristie inherits a heart, filled with dreams and love for Becky. A treasure. A part of me. A part of France. The enchanting country of castles and cafés.

The keepsake from a foreign land is more than enough to hold our lives together in strong, fierce loyalty. Becky's death will not separate us because our hearts will always find a place like Margie's where children carry on a mother's dream.

Come. Remember these watering places. If you dare take the plunge, the pure steam of the human spirit will satisfy your deepest longings. As Robert Frost concludes, "Drink and be whole again beyond confusion."

Something of Beauty

September 11, 1996

My friend Joann and I walked into downtown Romeo from her house. It had been too long since our last visit together. We ordered ice-cream cones and found a picnic table in the park to sit and talk. The summer's warmth surrounded us, insisting we twirl our cones to lick the melting sweetness.

The atmosphere was perfect: blue skies, the fragrance of fresh flowers and green grasses, and good food with a friend. But the climate of our souls was a cloudburst of emotions. This was not a meeting to discuss the light and happy details of life, but to support each other in our time of loss. And we did so gladly.

Joann washed my spirit with her gentle tears of compassion and sympathy. She has three daughters too, you see. They brought us together eight years ago. She told me, "I can't imagine your pain … how you face life without your Becky."

Her earnest effort to bear my burden lifted the darkness of my grief enough for me to see her needs. Unemployment fell upon her husband almost a year ago and persists. They have two daughters in college and one in high school. I asked how she was managing.

She shared with me their growth during distress. They discovered the positives and negatives buried in trials and tribulations. They have broken new ground. But she needs to see tangible fruit from the seeds of their hard work and faith. In the bleak midnight hour, she needs something of beauty to carry on to the finish. She explained how silly she felt about needing the bright cheerful faces of flowers in her window boxes. Her appetite for flowers was keener than ever.

I related. My gardens are groomed before my housework is done. We agreed hurting hearts search for something of beauty to soothe the sad circumstances of life. If it's not flowers, it's a new jumper or a splash of some little something new for the house.

I thought of my mission trip to the Ukraine three summers ago. The devastation of communism was evident in their housing structures, gray drab high-rises crowding two to four families in one apartment. The commercial districts were worn and barren. The people walked the streets with little clip in their steps. They waited in lines for their food in dirty depleted government stores.

But I saw flowers everywhere! The Ukrainians found beauty in their tiny gardens. Cosmos bloomed everywhere, proving communism couldn't convert the human need for beauty. They used the rich soil to grow the largest dahlias I've ever seen. With toothless smiles, little old women sold their beauties in booths along the streets. Almost every man and woman walked the sidewalks with arms full of fresh bouquets. They took their beauty home.

You will most likely find flowers on Joann's table, placed carefully as a testimony to her faith … her search for understanding, hope and peace.

I encourage you to allow the refreshing rain of your tears to water the flower of your soul. This is the beauty the lens of loss magnifies for us. Internal, eternal truth. We would not see it, we would not become it, without the journey through our waste places. There is no better companion. Nothing brings greater pleasure than something of beauty.

They Like Fruitcake

December 25, 1996

If you are searching for a controversial subject to discuss during a holiday gathering, just mention fruitcake, especially in a mixed group. Although fruitcake bashing is predictably popular during the holidays, this heavily battered dessert does have some merit.

Laying all the "brick" jokes aside, even the most hostile consumer would soften their opinion if they had pleasant fruitcake experiences built into their life. (I do recognize a fraternity of mankind who will never respect anything that resembles fruitcake. I respect that.)

If your mother could bake like my Southern mom, perhaps you wouldn't wince at the word "fruitcake." Baking was fun with Mom. Flour and sugar flew from floor to ceiling as we filled the turkey roaster with decorated cookies. Sweetness. But her fruitcakes didn't interest me or my four sisters back then. Fruitcake was safe with the adults.

My fruitcake taste buds developed sometime after I experienced childbirth. Could this be the mysterious milestone of fruitcake appreciation? Could this also explain the predominantly male contempt for the dense dessert?

At any rate, Mom's fruitcake recipe is followed annually with other traditional favorites in my household. Although our baking is greatly reduced this year, fruitcakes are a priority because Grandma and Grandpa Underwood enjoy them as gifts. (Oh, Grandma likes her without golden raisins.)

It seems as though my girls have been slipping into the fruitcake age a bit earlier than their mom. I first noticed it the night they stole the last piece of candied fruits and nuts off my plate when my back was turned. It was another one of those Kodak moments. The two of them (18 and 19 years old at the time) sat at the kitchen table with those mischievous eyes and guilty grins. Once their deed was discovered, they proceeded to fight over the last lump. I won. I take my tea and fruitcake seriously.

Then last week, Ruth (now 20) tackled me to take over the fruitcake batter. She grossed me out with her finger scoop into the dough, lifting out a chunk of pecans and candied cherries into her mouth. (Sorry, Grandma and Grandpa.)

Please understand these are not deprived young adults. They've sampled the more normal to finer sweets of life. Brownies, chocolate chip cookies, rocky road bars, pies and cakes to French and Austrian pastries. Who can figure their premature taste for fruitcake?

Not me. It delights me regardless because fruitcake is one of their few common tastes. Couldn't they have chosen to enjoy something together that causes greater ripples on the ocean of life ... greater peace and harmony in the home?

No. They like fruitcake.

Nonetheless, I am encouraged. For there is hope for other mutual tastes and interests if they can agree upon something as controversial as fruitcake.

Homeplace

January 1, 1997

Christmas Eve we drove the winding roads into the heart of the Appalachian Mountains to Mom's house. Phelps, Kentucky, is her home. Not too many people have ever heard of it. No wonder. It's rather remote.

Those tucked-away places hold my ancestry within their hills, hollers and bottoms. Sensing my roots wrapping their welcoming arms around me, I mentioned to my family the rich heritage I have as McCoy. Yes, the strong Irish and Scottish blood mixed to produce my mom, my dad and me.

My youngest daughter remarked she didn't have a heritage. How could growing up in Detroit and someplace between Romeo and Oxford, Michigan, possibly compare to my heritage? I explained to her my heritage was her heritage. I wasn't raised in Kentucky, but in Detroit and Warren, Michigan. But my childhood home was the mountains of Kentucky, every summer for a too-short vacation.

My husband drove the car down the *run-off*, the driveway into the McCoy Bottom. Home again—the place where I learned to walk and run. Sure enough, I am a purebred ridge-runner. The friendly ghosts of the old red barn, smokehouse and Uncle Herm's chickens appeared in the little valley. Connected again. The purity of my past nurtured me.

Mom opened her door at 11:45 p.m. to the Underwood clan. We walked into several days and nights of comfort and joy.

After Mom's delicious Christmas dinner, we walked next door to the farmhouse to visit Granny. At age 94, Granny was the furthest reaching living connector to our beginnings. Her strong heart beat against four years of confinement to her bed, and strokes rendered her once round figure feeble and thin.

Age closed her eyes to dim slits, and the strokes drew her mouth sideways. But her right hand remained full and healthy, as if it could whip up a batch of biscuits at moment's notice. Oh, how I longed to hear her words of wisdom once more! To hear her pray.

As Granny slept, the walls of the old house began to speak. They reminded me of my experiences with the house. As the phenomenon goes, the house seemed much smaller than my memory recollected.

I climbed the stairs (which seemed much taller as a child) to the upper hall and bedrooms. The first room to the right was my bedroom forty-five years ago, and contains my earliest childhood memory. Huddled in bed, Mom comforted me as we watched from my bedroom window the mountain across the road ablaze with fire. My daddy was on the flaming hill, and I was frightened for him. Thankfully, he made it home safe and sound.

Inspecting each room, I found Granny's cedar chest. The chest held her last will and testament—and much more. I sat on the chest and recalled the history of the old house—I saw the winding turns that led my Granny back home.

Granny's second marriage after Grandpa's death removed her from the farmhouse around 1949. My parents moved in for a brief time until they moved to Michigan when I was four—a long time ago.

Uncle Tab and Aunt Alma Leigh took occupancy after my parents and raised their family in the Homeplace. Those years are my fondest and richest. At age nine, I spent one barefoot summer month with them. My only regret is the changes they made to the house through remodeling. The wraparound porch was removed, taking much of the house's character to the woodpile, and burned.

Several long-term renters followed my aunt and uncle until recent vacancy permitted my Granny's return. My mom had the insight to move her mother back to her Homeplace for her last days.

The walls of her home spoke mysteries to me that I can never describe—mysteries of family and home. My heart swelled with love and devotion to my Granny and my mother for making me a home.

I returned to the room where my family gathered around Granny. How I longed for the walls of my heart to speak clearly like the walls of the Homeplace. How I desired to draw them into the intimacy of the rooms where our heritage thrives!

As Mom reminisced events, each story found their place in a chamber of my heart, adding to our heritage and holding our hearts together with invisible bonds. Bonds that will keep us joined when Granny is gone.

Mom plans to move to Florida after Granny's passing. Visits to the McCoy Bottom and the Homeplace may end. The winding road of life will lead my family and me other places. But I have courage for change. For the mountains live within my daughters and me, encouraging us to face the future with hope, for we carry home within us from destination to destination and generation to generation.

Yes, I trust we will always feel the pull home, to return to where we belong—this mysterious Homeplace, hidden in the hills, hollers and bottoms of our hearts.

The Magic Flute

January 29, 1997

Have you ever heard of James Galway?

He's a flutist, *par excellence.* Having had a brief interlude with the flute as an elementary student, I appreciated his command of and love for his instrument when I saw him perform on television years ago. The rich, fluid tones seemed to originate as much from his soul as the silver tube placed at his mouth.

Loving the soothing sound of the flute, I recently purchased Mr. Galway's CD, *The Wind Beneath My Wings.* It is mood-altering music, especially for the romantic, melancholy type. It's good medicine for the vexed soul and mind.

My oldest daughter, Becky, also took flute lessons in school for several years. She was a natural. But the discipline of practice cramped her style when sports and studies demanded more of her time. I all but bribed her to stick with it, but like her mom, her musical gift was sacrificed on the altar of immaturity.

But all was not lost, for Chris Vaneman lived next door. And he loved to play his flute. Chris was one year older than Becky and was very interested in music as a career. I never did see the flute to his mouth, or even in his hand, but my household knew he played because we heard the evidence.

This is what I remembered when listening to Mr. Galway's album. That same distinctive virtuoso floated from Chris's second-story bedroom window on invisible musical scales, filling our connecting lots on Algonac Street with his melodious talent. There were divine days of summer sonatas and honeysuckle breezes as I stood by my kitchen sink and drank the full cup of beauty. I lingered by screened windows when needy for another fresh anointing of the magic flute.

Kelly, home for a brief visit from college last night, also recalled Chris and Algonac as I shared my new CD with her. She spoke fondly of those childhood days, considering them "the best a kid could have." The Vanemans and Algonac are tied to our hearts with golden musical chords.

Kelly and I agreed it was a sad day when Karen (Chris's mom) informed us they were moving to the Lansing area. Life on Algonac just wasn't the same without our magic flute. We wondered what Chris was doing these days. Karen wrote in a Christmas card several years ago that Chris had married a flutist. Good idea. Wouldn't it be marvelous to hear the music they make together?

Louis Armstrong had said, "What we play is life." Yes, that's what Chris did. Musicians lift sorrow's heaviness from our broken hearts with their living music. And we listen again, and again, and again.

What provokes sweet musical memories from your human heart? For baby-boomers, "Chances Are" some golden oldie is the vehicle that takes you down memory lane. And Motown sounds will take you back to cruising McDonald's. I wonder how many shoes lost their soles to the Motown beat during those dancing days. Or is it some timeless classic like "Ode to Joy" that makes your spirit soar?

I'm most certain Chris never knew he refreshed me with the mysterious language of his flute—how he performed miracles on my discouraged soul and lifted me to places of divine worship at my kitchen sink. How, many times, his magic flute was the wind beneath my wings.

One Small Room

February 12, 1997

Angie and I were talking on the phone last week. Our friendship began seventeen years ago as we watched her Christa and my Becky run cross-country and track together. She is one of my rock-solid friends who has always made *being* real surprisingly easy. I don't know how she does it, but I'm so glad she does.

Angie spoke comforting words concerning my Becky's death. After some time, I shook myself from my self to remember her suffering. Angie and El (her husband) lost their thirty-year-old niece to cancer just months before Becky died. I inquired how her surviving nieces and sister-in-law were managing.

Angie's response revealed I had something in common with one of her nieces. My friend explained her niece has been sleeping in the bed where her sister died. I too have been crawling into the bed where Becky last slept in our home. This is normal for a season, I'm told. She said she believed we must permit each other to grieve in our own personal ways.

When Becky left home years ago, her small room was handed down to Kelly. When Becky returned home for her brief periods of sobriety, Kelly surrendered her room to Becky, uprooting her belongings for her sister's sake. Each return visit with us marked the room with lasting ambivalent scenes. Scenes that revive the conflict between hope for her recovery and the evidence against it.

I remembered my conversation with Angie the next time I pulled the comforter of Kelly's bed up to my chin. As I lay exhausted under the thick warmth, flashbacks of my father's last days were in the same little room. The last five days of his life were gifted to me in my home. Assisting him to bed after heart surgery. Bringing his medication to him in the night hours. Hearing his tender words of love to me in the same room where Becky slept. I wept the flood of memories, watering the comforter's petite flowers.

Understanding mingled with the tears as the darkness of night pulled the past into the present. Yes, this is why I must return to the room where my loved-ones last lived in my home. The room holds the life and love of my lost hopes and dreams for them. Kelly's bed is the compelling place where their memory lives. I will remain and mourn for them. I will wait until hope returns.

It's peculiar. When Kelly left for college four years ago, I found comfort in her room. I had grown so accustomed to seeing her study in her room that I found myself visiting her bed. Her character and spirit inhabited her room. Her tiny tap shoes danced into my mind as they hung on the shelf above her bed. Her salutatorian medallion hung in her honor next to her shoes. Her posters and pictures invited me to return to their places and times. And I did, confident that Kelly would be there.

Little did I know then that the beginning of my losses had begun. I was learning to release the ones I had held closely to me. Not just for a season, but into the hands of God for eternity.

And if I know Angie, she'll encourage her niece to grieve honestly until her season is accomplished. She'll watch carefully until her niece is able to let her sister go. Then she'll be right by her side to usher her into the season of hope.

Why am I so sure? Because Angie's heart is a lot like Kelly's room. It has experienced the loving and losing of precious life. To me, she is like my Comforter. She absorbs my cries with the warmth of her heart and draws me into the joy of hope.

Her heart holds an eternity of companionship and compassion. I don't know how she fits so much into one small room, but I'm so glad she does.

Why Mom's a Democrat

February 19, 1997

Christmas 1996 we gathered in the atmosphere of family, spending some time with our 94-year-old Granny who had been bed-confined for four years. I had returned *home* to Kentucky from Michigan with my immediate family to share the Holiday with Mom, who was Granny's caregiver.

Four female generations reminisced about life on the "McCoy Bottom." Grannies have a way of provoking such mining of memories. Especially our Granny. Her frank, Scotch-German wit and opinions were always predictable. There was no considering telling a fib around her. The truth was always to be spoken. Although her stern face was threatening, her round arms and dimply elbows were always free to hug her grandchildren.

As Granny slipped in-and-out of sleep, her presence dominated the climate of the room, causing confessions of childhood secrets. We revealed the silly notions that took root in our young hearts, growing unaware into adult judgments and fears. Each telling story bridged the generation gap as we sat before each other as little children.

The strong emotion of the moment directed Mom to a place in her past where she had never taken us before. My sister and her sons, and my daughters and I sat spellbound as Mom opened her heart. She told us of her love for her dad. We had heard this before, but his time she spoke with the fierce loyalty of a child.

She set the scene. Just a little girl, she lived in the farmhouse where we were all gathered. Her little baby brother had died. Sadness filled her house and heart. Her daddy had asked his brothers who lived across the creek to help him bury the baby. They refused. She remembers her daddy's thin frame and sorrowful eyes as he carried the little coffin on his shoulder away from the farmhouse. She could not bear the thought of him carrying the coffin by himself up the hill to the cemetery.

"Do you know why Dad's brothers wouldn't help him bury his baby?" Never before had Mom brought us so close to her suffering. There were various responses among her audience as we struggled to imagine how a family could abandon one of their own in his greatest hour of need.

"Because Dad voted for Roosevelt, that's why." Mom spoke with her inimitable stiff lower lip, attempting to maintain her emotions as she revealed the family secret. The words brought with them a deliverance from her prison of pain as we vicariously suffered her injustice.

"That's ridiculous! Why would voting for Roosevelt anger them?" We were unanimously incredulous.

She continued her story with confidence of our support. "Because they were Republicans. Dad and his brothers, all the relatives, had *always* voted Republican. When Dad voted that one year for Roosevelt, they rejected him and his family. The only time they had anything to do with Dad was when they needed something."

Again, we all agreed Grandpa's voting choice was no excuse for excommunication.

Mom confessed, "I remember being so angry at my uncles for how they hurt my dad. I wouldn't speak to them when they talked to me. Every time I saw one of my uncles, I saw my daddy carrying that little coffin on his shoulder. Finally, one day Daddy told me he noticed how unkind I was to my uncles and asked me why I wouldn't talk to them. So I told him.

"Daddy told me that I must forgive my uncles, that there would be no more of this disrespectful behavior. I tried to forgive them for my daddy's sake, but do you know..." Mom paused in reflection, as if a revelation had fallen into her heart.

"That's why I'm a Democrat. I could never be a Republican if it meant being mean like my uncles." Mom spoke with assurance and self-awareness, realizing she had stumbled upon a hidden childhood foundation stone. One that built within her life a judgment, similar to the one her uncles had made.

I can't speak for anyone else, but Mom's disclosure brought me a deeper understanding of who Grandpa was and who she is. She took the truth a step further than Granny, who, like most of her generation, found it very difficult to talk of hidden things.

I realized it is those hidden things that motivate our actions and cause us to hide ourselves from our family. If Mom had not confided her true self with her children, we would never have known what makes her the way she is.

In a moment of spontaneous honesty, we learned silly notions have serious origins in human experience. And we discovered why Mom was a Democrat.

The Apple Doesn't Fall Far

March 26, 1997

I just love Southern expressions. They're terse and entertaining. The history behind them is generally humorous and relates to the simplicity of daily life. I could sit and listen for hours to my relatives as they communicate with their unique language.

Southern front porches make excellent storytellers of those who rock in their swings and chairs. The listener is forced to develop patience when the teller pauses in typical Southern style. I've never been able to determine if the rest permits the teller time to adlib or gather true memories as they travel from generation to generation in their mind.

I remember hanging over the gaps between Uncle Tab's words while we shucked corn, tied up tomatoes or strung a "mess" of green beans together. We also ran "foot races" around the farmhouse when I was a kid. He was one of my heroes.

So was my Uncle Herm who always tells stories with a twinkle in his eyes. I've been told he's the one of my four uncles who most resembles the Grandpa I never knew. Among many things, he's my "blackburry" picking uncle. You should see him laugh when he tells the story about the day we were picking the "purdiest blackburries" you ever did see, when I happened upon a "wasper's" nest. Yes, he takes me back to the "blackburry" bushes with his with his expressions. I had never seen my "slow-as-molasses" Uncle Herm run as fast as he did on that mountain slope! And I was right on his heels!

A sweet swarm of those memories hovered over my sisters and me during the days we spent in Kentucky for Granny's funeral last week. The native idioms reconnected us to our heritage, warming the cold spots frozen by northern living. As often happens, we stumbled upon one that "took to us real fast" and "follerd" us throughout our visit at Mom's house.

My sister Sonia was discussing our mother's inherited gift of hospitality from our Granny. She concluded with emphasis, "The apple doesn't fall *fur* from the tree, ya' know." All of us present agreed in unanimity. I don't know if this expression is a Southern original, but considering the apple trees growing in Mom's backyard, and for the sake of this story, I'll allow Southern roots to claim it.

For instance, my sister Linda, the firstborn of five daughters, consistently insisted she was moving up from #3 in rank to Mom's #2 position, and Mom was replacing Granny as #1 boss. We all knew this was not an issue to be debated because we are well familiar with the authority with which Granny ruled, and how our mother is just like Granny.

Linda is a "spittin' image" of Mom. Yep, the apple didn't fall too "fur" from the tree. We know there's no sense in fighting the inevitable. My other sisters and I agreed to oblige Linda, and hope Mom lives a good, long life as #1 boss.

My sister Patty has lived in Kentucky for nearly 20 years. She married a Hatfield, which is humorous (or dangerous) because we are of McCoy stock. Patty invited us to stop by for breakfast on our way home yesterday morning. This was a bribe I couldn't refuse, because Patty makes the "purdiest" biscuits. And breakfast at her home means biscuits, gravy, eggs, sausage and fried apples.

Yes, Patty "cooked up" a pan of fried apples. My favorite. Granny introduced me to fried apples as a child. She showed me how to eat them on my buttered biscuits, "kinely" like miniature pies. *M-m-m-m*. The steamy smell of frying apples makes my mouth water. They "shore" are good!

After breakfast, we hugged and gave our good-byes. I thanked Patty for her hospitality and delicious meal. I told her she makes the best biscuits this side of Mom's house. She told me she was carrying on Granny's legacy. As long as she is able, she will offer what she has to those whom she loves.

The biscuits and gravy stuck to my ribs the many miles from Kentucky to Michigan, as did the richness of my heritage to my mind. Yes, you can take the girl out of the mountains, but you can't take the mountains out of the girl.

We all have inherited gifts and talents from our ancestors. We take pieces of them with us wherever we go. Their seeds live within us. We impart these seeds to our children and to those whom we love. The seeds grow into fruitful trees.

Yes, the expression is true. No matter where your tree is planted or transplanted, the fried apple doesn't fall "fur" from the tree.

Windy Season

April 9, 1997

The wind is blowing in a new season. Its roaring fury has the trees outside my window swaggering helplessly. With spring's greening comes the price of pushing winter aside. When the swirling wind hits my house in a certain way, the kitchen door whistles like my teapot.

I can predict spring's boisterous breath every year. My daughter Kelly was born on April 5, giving a great gauge to remember the weather. A few warm April days don't fool me, for there is always either an ice storm or silly snow in April. If not, snow is sure to fall in May. One year the snow missed May to flurry in June. Yes it did!

Believe the snow story or not, there is no denying the endurance of the wind. I have eaten dirt as it flew from the blades of the rotor-tiller to my mouth. I have cried in despair when the wind blew away acres of straw from our new yard of grass seed. This is when I'm tempted to give up. After months of winter's harsh treatment, June's calm, summer breezes seem out of my reach. Winter does not let go easily.

Life's elements had brought deep defeat to me last Saturday night. My hope of ever knowing joy as a companion again was dead. I was simply going through the motions of preparing for another holiday without my daughter, Becky. Balancing life against death, responsibility against grief, I longed to enjoy my family and express my love for them.

I prayed for mercy. I willed to hold fast to whatever shred of faith I possessed. It would be enough. It must.

On our drive to church the next morning, a sense of blessing touched me as I remembered Christ's death, burial and resurrection. I expressed to my family my thankfulness for His sacrifice. The spoken words released a gentle hope to encourage my heart.

The remainder of the day was not without sorrow and the challenge of controlling such sadness, but hope hung tightly to me as we prepared dinner and made our traditional Bunny cake. There was just enough strength to make it through the day.

A recent call from my Massachusetts friend, Dotty, gave perspective to my Easter experience. She spoke her usual words of wisdom and comfort. "Iris, take one day at a time. God gives you strength for only one day at a time. Do you remember what you told me years ago?"

I was afraid to ask.

"You told me our will is stronger than our emotions."

"Dotty, I didn't tell you that."

"Yes you did! And it's true. I'm proof!"

My own words were gritty in my mouth like the dirt from my garden. The winds of change had blown them into my face.

And Dotty was right … as usual. I had willed to hold fast to my faith and my family. Hope resulted. I confess: I don't like that order.

I struggle with death, especially the death of my daughter. Her death has blown away so much life. But death will happen. It must, for rebirth to occur.

The trillium die every winter, but return every May. Yes, I remember the white petals of the woodsy trillium. The wind cannot blow them away. Their roots are deep within the earth, like Dotty's.

Be sure, we will sway in the tempestuous seasons. We will drink from many bitter cups before we can sit and sip sweet, tall glasses of summer's iced tea.

Someday the winds will cease. All that the winds haven't blown away will bloom and color the earth. For resurrection power is stronger than the weather. It is stronger than death.

The seed is in the earth. We will see it again. Yes, I will hold to my faith. I believe there is life after death.

Sweeping Vistas

July 2, 1997

As a lover of words, it is not unusual for me to be mesmerized by certain combinations of our alphabet which seem to have an anointing upon them. Symbols are transformed into glorious and gracious language to take us places our five senses cannot. When anointed words meet with anointed places, their marriage produces pure poetry. Creativity thrives. The human spirit soars above understanding and limitations to see the invisible and dream the impossible.

I was surprised today, once again, by the beauty of words. A phone call from a friend took me to a *beyondness* with her words.

She called me to invite me to a tea she is hosting for a small group of women from our art appreciation class. That's where I met Lisa. We women bonded there by the elements of art and the skill of our excellent teacher. At semester's end, we decided to continue our friendship.

So we did at my house a few Fridays ago with our first tea to honor our teacher. During the phone conversation, Lisa reminisced her favorite moment of that particular afternoon.

We were in the agreeable June outdoors. Gentle breezes blew over the rolling hills in rhythm to the strumming of our teacher's guitar. Lisa confessed she wrote down on paper her strong reflections of the experience, but felt foolish and destroyed them.

"Oh no!" I responded. For as she spoke, Lisa took me back to the moment in time of sweeping vistas. Her pure heart and poetry quickened the far-reaching mental view of my backyard. The words "sweeping vistas" stopped my mind for a visit of revival.

The powerful effect of the word "vistas" swept my memory to Linda and Ron's (a sister and brother-in-law)

Vista Cruiser, their old station wagon. We were young families then, before mini-vans were on the scene. The Vista Cruiser was in our lives long enough to build a great fondness for it.

One summer, we packed aunts, uncles and cousins (a total of eleven, and three baby car seats) in the ol' Vista Cruiser. We snaked through the mountains of Kentucky from Mom's house toward home, soaking in the sights as Ron turned the steering wheel from scene to scene. The kids remember the Vista Cruiser. It is preserved in snapshots and super-8 family film.

Yes, Lisa's words moved me from one place to another. That's the wonder of words coming from a pure heart. They conceive truth that transforms the ordinary into the extraordinary and the mundane into the marvelous. Heart words are traveling troubadours, singing the concert of creation.

I asked Lisa to rewrite her words for me. They are pregnant with meaning, giving birth to gentle yet powerful life. They quickened life to me. They placed my fingers on the pulse of the past. They swept me away from the gray cubicles, glass walls and economic forecasts of an office building to vistas unseen by the natural eye.

Dear reader, I encourage you to deliver the words you have conceived. Write them down. Look at them. Touch them with your fingertips. Feel their pulse.

Birth the truth. It may look foolish at first, but it possesses the energy of life. In time you will become comfortable with your new freedom to write. You will soon learn to be carried away on the wind of sweeping vistas.

Beauty for Ashes

July 16, 1997

These long summer days are too short ... especially days like yesterday and today. The extended daylight is not enough time to enjoy the stored-up anticipation accumulated during winter's hibernation.

Yesterday at work, employees gathered at the 12th floor window of the Chrysler Tower. Overlocking the I-75 traffic under a promising blue sky, they were doing the TGIF countdown. I wasn't included in their group, but my spirit was standing with them, just the same.

I planned the remains of the day on my drive home. A walk on this fair evening was a must. Changed into my good ol' grubbies and bounding toward the driveway, I spied my neighbor filling a birdfeeder. She accepted my invitation to join me.

As we crunched the dirt road under our feet, we quickly caught up on the events of the week. Our skin tingled at the refreshing cool spot in the road by the old dairy farm. Peggy's childhood memories surfaced like our goosebumps when we confessed how fond we were of the dilapidated barn ... a monument to the fading agrarian lifestyle.

She spoke of the days her parents transported their nine children from their Detroit home to an uncle's dairy farm in Caseville. The kids played themselves bone-tired. Their uncle tied a rope in the barn and stacked bales of hay for a tall swinging launch. They wore hooded sweatshirts so the cow-slobber wouldn't drip on their heads when they crawled under the cows during their milking. They squealed when the weird cow's tongue licked their faces. They didn't like *that*, but they loved the farm. Cows and all.

The halfway mark of our walk turned Peg and me west, toward home. Beauty stopped us in our steps. While we faced east, the invisible hand of the Almighty had silently streaked the sky with pinkish orange sunset chalks.

I told Peg about the last time I witnessed a comparable spectacle. A solitary May walk on the same road had prompted a prayer for my Becky. I had not heard from her in some weeks and was pouring forth my petitions for her safety. The sight of the swirling pink promise of summer, high above me, encouraged my heart.

Upon my return home, Becky phoned from Atlanta, Georgia. She was training for a new job and needed encouragement. We had a positive, heartwarming conversation. She gave me hope for her recovery to sobriety and family. But she couldn't get it together … she never made it home.

Peg shed a tear with me as she replied with a quivering smile, "But she painted the sky for you."

Yes, Peggy, who is very familiar with suffering, knows how to find beauty in ashes. She is a companion who walks with me through the valleys and stands by my side on the mountaintop.

Although our walks have been few and far between, Peg and I walk in each other's shoes daily. We bear one another's burdens. When one stumbles, the other gently supports. And on occasion, we steal a moment to enjoy the goodness that sorrow and busy lives camouflage.

Someday the future may lead Peg and me down different roads. But nothing can separate us because we have been fed by Beauty's breast. We are kindred spirits.

We have seen Queen Anne's lace blooming along the side of the road, and smiled at the nursing calves as they snuggled close to their mother. We have greeted the first star of the night together.

O weary and lonely soul, remember your companions. Trust God's light by day and night to guide you into rest. Take time to lean your head on Beauty's breast and be nourished by the sweet milk of His love song.

A Silver Lining

August 13, 1997

I received the most unusual invitation last summer. My mom, Sadie McCoy, asked me to join her for her class reunion dinner/dance. "I'd love to be your date!" I replied. What better way to learn about Mom than from former classmates? I couldn't wait to see her in action. I've not seen her dance in years.

The five-hundred-mile drive from Michigan to Kentucky in mid-July offered time for much reflection. Many childhood memories of the trip south with Mom played back like tapes in my mind. My transplanted mother returned to the place of her roots every summer for over twenty years, taking her young family (and sometimes reluctant husband) with her.

Her move back *home* after a divorce lured me and my young family south for a generation. But this trip was different. My children had grown and I was alone—and loving it. The quiet allowed me to absorb and observe the turns in the road and landscape as never before. And when I saw the distant range of the Appalachians at that certain point of the Mountain Parkway when the mountains first come into view, my heart leaped with excitement. I felt like a girl again, surprised by a friend who sneaked up on me and tickled my sides.

Mom's Kentucky home was filled with out-of-town guests when I arrived just hours before the dance. The Phelps High School reunion brought folks from far and near.

Herb and Eleanor (brother and sister) are Mom's childhood friends. Their brother, Stanley, was one of Mom's high-school sweethearts. He was killed in WWII. Herb and Eleanor put faces on names Mom has dearly mentioned on numerous occasions. The past merged with the present.

Cousins I had never met found refreshment in Mom's cool kitchen. They talked about family and friends who were only names to me. My excitement grew as I anticipated meeting new faces.

Classmates from the '30s to '60s crowded into the high school's cafeteria for dinner. My aunts and uncles were surprised to see me as Mom's escort. What fun it is to be unconventional!

During dinner, a man remarked that a certain woman was "full of her self." It seems some things never change. It's easy to imagine the same scene some decades ago: school cafeteria, boy and girl. Boy looks at girl; sizes her up; announces his score.

The band began before we finished dessert—and they never stopped (but to tell bad jokes). The local musicians cranked out decent danceable tunes of all kinds.

Age had not disguised two familiar faces from my childhood visits south. Janey and Kitty were classmates of my cousin, Kathy McCoy. I ran "run-offs" and the "bottom" every summer vacation with my "cuz."

Kitty and her three sisters joined hands in a jitterbug circle. They linked the past to present, picking up where they left off. That happens at reunions.

My aunts, uncles and cousins jitterbugged with the best of 'em. I could have watched cousin Eat-a-bee (Edith Marie) dance all night. But my favorite dance was the one dedicated to my mother. My cousin Paul held Mom's hand close to him and honored her with the Righteous Brother's "Unchained Melody." My beautiful mom swished around the dance floor in her graceful, fluid colors. Her hair was like a silver crown of nobility.

I wondered if Stanley were alive, would he be her dance partner? Would she have married my dad? Would I be here tonight? Reunions get you to thinkin'. Thinking of what might have been. But you can't be reunited to what might have been.

I left Mom in Paul's good hands and drove alone to her home under a full, mountain moon ... the same moon that led Mom safely home from school over sixty years ago.

The same moon I was born under in Matewan, West Virginia.

The silvery moon mist fell softly like a diaphanous veil upon the dark mountains, intoxicating me with a sense of well-being. The mountains spoke to me once again in a gentle whisper, "Welcome home."

I felt the pull of the tide that separates and unites, separates and unites: mother and daughter, husband and wife, sisters and brothers, friends. And this never-ending cycle will again separate and reunite the classmates. They will blend again into one group to celebrate their common bond.

But seldom does a reunion happen without human intervention. They are work. They require energy, initiative, and sometimes courage. Courage to face change. Courage to face sameness.

Reunion is separation's silver lining. How could we bear the pain of separation without the hope and joy of embracing our beloved once again? As long as my mother lives, I will leave and return, leave and return.

Our invitations for reunion may present themselves in many forms: earnest eyes of repentance, spoken or written confessions, or lighthearted engagements. Whatever the case, reunion is worth the effort. It is worth the risk.

What better way is there to enjoy life than to be joined once again to those who have been separated from us? Ah, to dance with joy to the sweet harmony of reunion! And to drink of the goodness of home from a cup filled with Kentucky moonshine.

A Snake in My Toilet

August 20, 1997

Sometimes this world offers the most unusual happenings in the most unexpected places. A Michigan mid-summer's tea was the setting: a lace tablecloth, a vase of freshly cut roses, elegant dishes, fragile crystal glasses, a crispy clean kitchen and a petite young Martha Stewart making it happen.

The flavors of the spinach quiche, orange bread and fruit torte were equal to the ambiance. The blend of exterior support inspired superior human communion. We guests absorbed the Victorian personality of our hostess's home. We felt honored to be served with such detailed attention.

Fairly new friends, we four discussed our likes and dislikes concerning literature, movies, art and our families. As discussions go, ours went the way of diversion. One friend spoke of her dislike for spiders and snakes. Another asked if we had heard about the pet snake that had escaped and was at large.

We responded we had not heard of any runaway reptile. Our friend proceeded to give the information as she recalled the news report. Whatever kind of snake it was, it supposedly was hiding in a local bog. The most alarming news was the disappearance of neighboring pets.

We all agreed a rebellious snake is not something we would want to encounter—in our gardens or otherwise. The guest who introduced the spider and snake subject said that she has heard of snakes finding their way into toilets via sewer systems. She confessed she keeps her toilet lids down—just in case.

I shuddered at this "X-File-ish" scenario. I don't like snakes either. But we soon left the snake report and finished our afternoon together in light and lovely conversation. The clean, white refreshment of our hostess's house impressed me. The splashes of color in tiny accents lured my senses to very nook and cranny. I took home with me the view from her kitchen window — white picket fences and vining flowers over arbors. The rich green contrast showing through pure white lace curtains.

My most enchanting happening was the greeting from a lacy panel of an open window, waving gracefully by the breath of the summer breezes. Yes, the intimacy of friendship was inviting me again to linger and listen. The atmosphere was like a fine perfume.

The fragrance of the scenes encouraged me to care for my neglected house. The next day I dusted, vacuumed and polished my dwelling. I pruned houseplants and filled vases with cut flowers from my gardens.

And when it came to toilet-cleaning time, I couldn't help but chuckle at the snake story the previous day. Yes, I put the lid down. How peculiar … the run-away snake came home with me too.

But I did not fret. I've learned not to listen to the voice of the deceiving serpent. I'm wise to his lies. He's been hanging around for a long time. If he can't scare me in my garden, he'll try my toilet!

Nope, I'm going to think on whatever is lovely and pure. I close my eyes and see a curtain's blowing grace. I see friends gathered around a table set with love, hope and cheer.

Dancing Scenes

September 3, 1997

On this Labor Day, September 1, 1997, there is a predominant summer scene that surfaces like cream on un-homogenized milk. Among my encounters with speaking breezes, newborn grandnieces and America's waves of grain, a dance ever moves in my mind. Yes, Kelly dances before them all, leading with praises and adoration in summer's glory.

It was our first outdoor worship service of the season. My grown-up little girl danced before our God and me with her bare arms gracefully uplifted. Her straw hat held the sun in rich, honey hues. Although her back was to me, I knew she was smiling because Kelly delights in dancing. She always has.

She was unashamed. She had nothing to hide.

Joy lifted and landed her feet from Granny's quilt. The tiny flowery print on her dress moved in flowing agreement to the music's rhythm.

I danced with her. I had nothing to hide.

We have always danced. My three female toddlers had a pre-bedtime ritual. After their bath, they danced naked through our little bungalow. I chased them down with *jammies* in hand.

It was so much fun. They had nothing to hide.

As they grew, we progressed to leaps and tour-jetés. Alas, my living-room lessons gave way to Miss Diane who taught tap and ballet. Kelly was a "groovy chicken" with her little sister, Ruth. Their yellow tutus and feathers are fixed on photos. Becky, the oldest, danced a '50s number in a poodle skirt. Hilarious memories.

Kelly was a dancing solo snowflake in a white chiffon costume and silver glitter headpiece two-feet wide. She danced her little heart out before thousands of people. What courage at age eight!

Why not? She had nothing to hide.

I missed Kelly's ninth-grade *Annie* dance. I was in Vienna at the time, waltzing with Mel and Ruth.

But Kelly forgave me with "Hi Mom" on the seat of her bloomers in *The Wizard of Oz*. Whether center stage as Oliver, or a small part on the side, Kelly simply loved dancing.

I watched her dance with her sister at a wedding one Christmastime. We danced the "hustle" together.

We loved every minute. We had nothing to hide.

Last night, by the dancing flames of a family bonfire, Kelly told of their (her sister and cousins) escapades at a Royal Oak dance club. Her cousin Nathan laughed as he explained their fun with a wig.

He wore the long, brown thing as a gag to humor his three female cousins who flocked him on the dance floor. Scowling heads turned his way, unaware of the innocent fun intended. Those young men who were dressed to the hilt, watching from the balcony in serious attempt to spot their prey, hissed at Nathan's appearance.

Nate and his cousins enjoyed the irony of their fun. They had nothing to hide.

As I watched my American flag dance in the breezes today, a sense of freedom touched me. Liberty to lay down my burdens … to have the guts to have fun like my kids.

I realized all living things dance. Birds dance in a puddle of water in my driveway. Bees dance in pollination inside my flowers. The waves dance in the wake and spray of my sister's water skis.

They have always danced. They have nothing to hide.

And my Kelly's feet will always dance, and her soul shall always sing. If I watch and listen closely, I will learn lessons for *Tomorrow* and find *Where is love*.

Dear reader, let's carefully place our summer memories where they can easily be seen. Let's respond to the their call to liberty, "Please, come dance with me!" Let's answer, "Yes, I will dance with you. I have nothing to hide."

When I Get Old

September 17, 1997

I spent the bulk of the weekend abusing my flabby muscles because I enjoy gardening and the blooming results. Summer's end brings heavy-duty projects (transplanting space-greedy shrubs, take-over irises and hiding hydrangeas).

After five hours of "in-the-dirt grunt work," my hands started to tremor and my back was weaker than usual. "Wait a minute," I coached myself, "you used to work from 9 to 9 on Saturdays without even breaking for lunch! Don't quit till the job is done."

Pausing to survey the ground unfinished, my body told me exactly how tired it was. Even my tough mental attitude couldn't find the strength to stick it out. The job would wait until Sunday afternoon. So I threw in the shovel and made a beeline for a soak in a hot tub.

This has been my ritual for the past several years, as I feel age creeping up on my backside. A steamy, sudsy soak is my treatment for preventing total muscle rebellion. So, I obliged. It's the only way my body agreed to move out of bed this morning.

While tearing tubers apart and listening to the summer sounds today, an encounter with old man several Marches ago came to mind. I met him at a hospital where I was training telecommunications. After standing for several hours, I anticipated a rest. I strolled my swollen feet down the hall to the cafeteria for a soothing cup of hot tea (not to soak my feet, but to drink).

The cafeteria was in the process of remodeling and there were no food or beverage instructions for visitors. Having previously learned "the ropes," I was anxious to retrieve my tea and return to my quiet room and prop up my feet.

But a little old man shuffled in front of me, examining the huge stainless steel coffee urns. He moved as slow as molasses in (a Michigan) March. My impatience piqued as I shifted in my shoes. He handled several knobs unsuccessfully, obviously needing some assistance. Finally, I forgot my feet and asked if I could help him.

"Sure can! Just can't figure these things out."

"I know what you mean. It took me a time or two. It's the strangest coffeepot I've ever seen. May I carry your tray for you?"

"Sure. I'm only 92 years old, you know." Pride brought a youthful spark to his dim eyes.

"You're not!" I was impressed.

"One of these days, when I get old, I'm going to slow down." He looked into my eyes as he spoke. Safely escorted to his table, we said our good-byes.

My tea and reflections of the old man were good companions. I chuckled at his perspective. He didn't notice he indeed had slowed down. As a matter of fact, according to my pace, he couldn't have been much slower. But his playful practice kept his mind young and moving.

"You're only as old as you think." Is this a cliché or the truth? The old man possessed the spirit of a child. His body could not convince him that he was old. *I* would not dare. To do so would be cruel.

Today the wind carried the voices of generations to my garden. Children and parents laughing and playing together … a continuous cycle of life. I was a child, now I am a parent. Hopefully, if I live to be 92, I'll be on my feet too.

In the meantime, the old man reminds me to appreciate every stiff step to and from my gardens, no matter how slow the stride. While I'm getting old, I hope I remember to look into the eyes of the young and impatient and encourage them to take time to smell the coffee. As I learn the senior citizen shuffle, I hope I remember, as a woman thinks, so is she.

A Picture of Change

September 24, 1997

A picture says a thousand words.

Did you automatically associate Kodak with their ingenious slogan? Did a photo form as a mental picture? Yes, Kodak knows their business. For photo fans like myself, most every closet and available drawer in the house is stuffed with pictures. Someday, they will all be chronologically entered into albums.

But it seems to me Kodak's promotional quip needs an alteration. Doesn't a picture express much more than words?

My daughter Ruth (20 years old) illustrates my point. She has inherited my appreciation for frozen faces in frozen places. Her bedroom walls and dressers are collage covered, giving a history of her life and relationships. Many of the framed pictures are from photo-loving friends; others are her creation. They all blend into a melting milieu, capturing the past for present visits.

There is one plain plastic frame designated as "the picture of the week, month, or whenever Ruth decides to change it." I have secretly enjoyed her choices as they reveal who and what she considers important. The photo is the highlight of the comfortable clutter covering her drafting table (which has never been used for drafting … yet).

Last week I noticed Ruth had changed her photo again. I realized her picture practice is telling of her personality. She's constantly changing her mind. She bores quickly with sameness. She's very visual.

The latest photo replacement was snapped over three years ago when Becky (Ruth's oldest sister) was alive. Nana, Pat (Becky's boyfriend), and Nathan (Ruth's cousin) joined the five Underwoods for a picture at Nathan's graduation party. It is indeed a keeper. Her younger sisters surround beautiful Becky. Nana looks tremendous too. Everyone is all smiles.

To think the picture almost didn't happen! It is work to corral a group into cooperation! Many emotions, relationships, hopes, dreams, goals and changes are represented in Ruth's "picture of the week." Generations birthing change every moment of every day. The challenge of living through losing Becky … to name a few.

As I studied the photo, I could see Ruth had changed. She was maturing. The picture spoke something to my mother's heart. I couldn't see it. It was sensed otherwise.

The next morning, we left the house before sunrise to drive Kelly (Ruth's older sister) to the airport for her flight to San Francisco. Yes, I took pictures of Kelly before she left the house. But I forgot the camera in the car at the airport! Nonetheless, I captured in my mind the picture of Kelly's eager, adventurous eyes as she turned to board the plane. Life was changing before my eyes.

Ruth sat next to me on our return home. She attempted to cheer me with her gregarious optimism. I would not. Change was forcing loss upon me again. I didn't expect Ruth to understand when I couldn't.

Since that morning, I have remembered the picture of Kelly's eyes. I can see Ruth's wide smile as we drove into the blinding goldness of the rising sun. The pictures of their face tell me change happens, but growth is optional. Am I going to grow with them, or apart from them?

Ruth will soon set her sails. The course of change will chart new seas for her. I can see her growth. She is preparing for that "farewell." And I am sure to snap the event.

Kelly and Ruth's "farewell" pictures will join Becky's on my desk. Like Kodak, I know my business. I AM a mother, and will be until I die. That is one thing that will never change. If I continue to listen to my children, I can grow with them. If they continue to hear my heart, they can grow with me.

Yes, Mr. Kodak, a picture says more than words. It conveys a thousand messages to our soul. Pictures tell how we have changed … how we have grown. They connect us to who we were, to who we are, and to who we are going to be.

But most importantly, a picture leaves a sixth sense of us behind for those who love us.

Passages

October 2, 1997

Becky's suitcases sat in my bedroom from the July day they were returned to us — without our daughter. It seemed sacrilegious to remove or even touch them. I knew it would take more strength than I possessed to intrude upon my child's personal belongings.

Her large gray suitcase sat against the cedar chest I bought her for a graduation gift. Her garment bag and a red box, holding some miscellaneous childhood treasures, joined the group of lonely orphans.

I remembered the stories of women who confessed their difficulty in parting with the clothing of their deceased husband or child. What counsel they brought my affliction! I wondered if they had the same dreams about their loved one returning as they had always before. Could this be why we protect their remnants from trespassers?

But Becky wasn't coming home. Three months had passed since her death, and my bedroom needed to be cleaned. So I planned for two days to move her suitcases to the basement. Thinking I had the courage, I approached to lift the gray suitcase, the graduation gift to Becky from my mother. Given in hopes for many happy travels and returns. The garment bag had to be removed first because it covered the suitcase. The unzipped bag exposed some clothing.

When my hands touched her garments, a gush of grief released, as if waiting for its cue. All I could voice was, "My baby, my baby," as I clutched each petite piece, smelling it, examining it for some trace of Becky's breath. None. Her beautiful legs and arms didn't fill the pants and blouses she once animated with her inimitable bouncy body. The torture was unbearable, so I zipped the garment bag, concealing the lifeless evidence.

I forced myself to continue as I piled the garment bag on the red box. Laying over the mound in pleas for mercy, I lifted my burden and left the room for the stairs and basement. Resolutely returning to the bedroom, I anointed the gray suitcase with my tears as we took the short journey downstairs.

It was finished.

My bedroom doesn't look or feel right. The sad ceremony left it empty and me filled with depression. I miss my companions. My reminders of my sweet Becky.

I have been inaugurated into the deeper ranks of the mourner's association. It is a forced membership, like the day an adolescent girl first learns about menstruation. Are we ever fully prepared for these passages of life and death? What would we do without our personal pioneers to encourage and counsel us?

I am told Becky's orphans will wait for our return. Someday, her sisters and I will open the suitcases together and handle the emptiness again. Three are better than one.

There are some passages in life and death we can postpone for a while, but they will not tarry for our approval or preparedness indefinitely. They stand at the door of our heart, waiting to weave us through eternal hallways that lead us into the sacred chambers of a loved one's memories.

Canning Tomatoes

October 22, 1997

I walked past bushels of tomatoes as I entered Harvest Time fruit market. *Mmmm* ... the smell of the red ripeness smacked my mouth with invisible flavor, causing me to taste a tomato, mayo and cheese sandwich. (I am devouring one as I write.)

Yes, tons of tomatoes are harvested this time of year in Michigan—another sign of fall. Tasty tomatoes are plentiful. We stuff ourselves, knowing the long winter season brings tasteless hothouse things that only resemble tomatoes. My mom, a tomato expert, refuses to eat them. They are not the *real* thing.

BLT's are also a seasonal treat, with a thick slice of tomato to escape and land on your lap or drip its juice on your shirt. Mom taught me to enjoy a meaty tomato with green beans and cornbread. Talk about de-lish!

I haven't grown tomatoes in years. Too busy with my flower gardens, I guess. But if I liked fried green tomatoes, my neighbors would willingly supply them. Their tomato plants are presently bare of leaves and loaded with green tomatoes, clinging to the vines in hopes our Indian summer will ripen them.

My taste for tomatoes was developed as a kid. Since Kentucky's long growing season ripens tomatoes in July, Mom's canning jars joined us for our summer vacations south. My family lived in Michigan most of my childhood, but we returned *home* when the gardens were *in*. Granny was happy to share her surplus tomatoes, bragging on the bumper crop her little plot provided.

Her hefty "Hunt" arms hauled huge pots of tomatoes to her kitchen sink where she dumped them. She poured boiling water over the tomatoes, making a steamy bath to soak their skins loose for peeling. I can still see her wipe the steam from her face as the heat provoked a fan of relief with the kitchen towel. It was one of Granny's own peculiar ways of doing things. She kept the kitchen towel on her broad shoulder, then took it with both hands for another fanning every now and then. I don't know how she endured the southern heat and humidity back then without air-conditioning. I can't ever remember hearing her complain.

Sometimes, in a quiet moment, I heard the skins splitting on the tomatoes. The smell of stewing tomatoes eventually filled the house and escaped out the kitchen windows into the alley and onto the porches (where we kids spent most of our time on the swing, avoiding the work). Granny would plunge her fat callused fingers into the boiling water, pull out a tomato and skin it in lightning speed. She cut it in sections and packed it into a sterilized canning jar.

This is where I helped. (Remember the old "Shake and Bake" commercial? The little Southern girl says about the chicken, "And I helped.") My skinny little hand fit perfectly inside the empty canning jars, with room for scouring corners. The jars were full of dead (and sometimes living) bugs of all Southern kinds.

The fruit cellar, by evidence of her canning jars, was *the* creepiest place in Granny's house. We grandkids dared not enter this formidable dungeon. Just recently, after her death, I entered Granny's fruit cellar with Mom to survey the remains of Granny's (and my) past, thus dismantling a mysterious room of my childhood. I left the sooty cellar much older.

But my Granny and my mom have preserved forever the sharp smell of canning tomatoes. I can remove these "together" memories from the dusty shelves of my mind and taste them again and again. I can return to the innocence and mystery of childhood by means of their legacy.

For they drew me into their lives through their love, devotion and darn hard work. I became a part of them, and they of me. I will pass on their legacy to my daughters by preserving it in words. All it takes is a bushel of tomatoes at

Harvest Time; soak them in my memory, peel them with devotion and process them with my computer.

And there you have it, Mom! The *real* thing to taste again and again.

Sitting with Sages

October 24, 1997

I have always needed to be included. Whether it is my family, neighborhood packs, or school organizations, I enjoy group participation. As a kid, the torture of waiting to be chosen was worth the rescuing rush I felt when added to the team.

Sure, there were times when I was left to last, standing alone in testimony to undesirability. Evidently, there was no permanent harm done, for I persisted in joining groups galore — finding fun and responsibility in healthy balance.

My athletic energy took a dive into my high school's synchronized swim club (even though I couldn't swim) and the cheerleading squad. My dramatic flair put me on stage while my civic mind established me in the student council.

Having a familial sisterhood, I didn't need a sorority during my college days. I found my *rush* from other groups. My "bucket mouth" (a nickname given by my high-school typing teacher) continued to cheer for the CMU Chips. What fun!

Motherhood delivered my time and interests into organizations typical to training three very ambitious daughters. Co-op preschools, church groups, gymnastic clubs … so many worthy ways to spend one's time and use one's talents. Did my girls need all that activity, or did I? I was caught up in the age of the *Super Mom*. And I was destined to be included in their ranks.

It wasn't until my third daughter that I learned to slow down a bit … just a bit. She was the only child home her last two years of high school. Why didn't I see the blue-bird of happiness flying into my empty nest?

My nest has burs of ambivalence, causing discomfort at times. And oddly enough, this is good. Yes, it is good to leave the familiar and transfer my energies to new places. But where?

In contrast, maturity is developing an increasing need for privacy. In the process of growing up, my need to be included is being adjusted. Staying home alone on a weekend night is no longer an insult. But yet, what I would give for a boring game of Scrabble with one of my girls (or my sister Sonia)!

In the midst of this transition, last month a friend invited me to the Oxford Rotary as a guest. She encouraged me to consider membership, assuring me of her positive civic and professional experiences with the organization. "We need a writer," she said.

The traditional "welcome" song (by predominantly male voices) was the best part of my first visit. Picture grown men singing a cutesy song to a female. Hilarious. They warned me the last person they sang to didn't return (their standard disclaimer).

But I returned because I felt comfortable. Sort of like my high-school student council days, but on a grander scale. The guys and gals have grown up, and some of them are senior citizens … some fought in WWII. My friend placed me at the "older fellows" table, as she called it. She told me I would just love them. I listened to their wisdom (and bad jokes). I laughed with them in their bantering.

How strange it felt. A good strange. The sages of Oxford were filling a need left by my father in his death. A need to sit at the feet of the elderly and learn from them … to hear again the ageless principles of community.

But their ideology is different from the Confucian scholars. The Oxford sages believe in freedom and equality for (wo)mankind. How do I know? They accept me as their equal. No, they don't bind my feet as the ancient Chinese sages did to every female child for its lifetime. They don't restrict my growth, but promote it. They lift me up to sit at their side. They encourage my achievement.

It is a high privilege to sit with the wise and gain from the mysterious transfer of experience and wisdom. To advance to another stage of my life under such great influence.

My friend was right. I do just love sitting with the sages—those old birds who make my empty nest a more pleasant place to live.

Caught between the Sun and
the Moon and Mozart

November 5, 1997

Have you ever felt like refusing to get out of bed and face the world? Be honest, now. Haven't we all had days like that? We feel like smashing the alarm clock when we hear the annoying buzz ... or reply with a murmuring "Oh, shut up!" to the voice on the clock-radio. This is exactly how I woke last Friday morning.

Every ounce of my week's supply of energy was spent by Thursday night. I knew when my head hit the pillow I was in trouble. My mind was mush (which is too firm a description). I couldn't even think of my 8 o'clock sign language class the next morning. Dyslexia was causing great frustration. My brain was slipping again, refusing to receive the messages. I dreaded the challenge of my disabilities.

I dreaded overhearing the younger students in my classes talk about getting drunk at their weekend parties. I dreaded the manipulation of political correctness within academia. Longing to finish this season of school in my life, I whimpered a prayer for a refreshing rest and sank into my bed.

Only a strong will was left to lift me out of bed when the alarm rang at 6:15 a.m. Going through the motions, my car headed south on Rochester Road for another day in the trenches. Oh, thank God it's Friday, I thought, thank God for Mozart, as I pushed the plastic cassette into the radio's mouth.

The eastern sky rippled with seashore clouds. The sunrise hinted at the horizon, making a celestial peach ocean. As the sun rose, its rays reached further into the sky, painting the clouds in perfect rhythm to Mozart's measures.

Within moments, the circle of sun was fully drawn, casting color almost as far as my eyes could see. Misty streaks of pink and peach hung over my head, greeting me as only the Divine can ... in perfect harmony with the music.

Mozart's timeless music and the rising of the sun lifted me out of my car to join in the celebration of another day. My mortal limitations could not keep me bound to Earth. My spirit soared on the strings of the violin and danced on the clouds. The *Timeless* filled my car and the atmosphere above me.

Turning my car westward, the moon smiled down upon me from the blue sky. My heart leaped. Within seconds, my spirit was caught between the sun and the moon. Morning and Evening met me ... caressed me. Time vanished. The ageless art of Creation gave me a glimpse of truth. And it is not found in time. Schedules and clocks do not regulate it.

The pinks had faded from the sky when I reached the parking lot at Oakland University. With great thanksgiving for my morning greeting, I bound up the stairs to my class. Humming Mozart to myself, I sensed the Son had fully risen in my heart.

O dear reader, what a good God we have! He heard the weak whine of one of His children and answered with majestic voices. Mozart alone could have revived me. But no, the Sun also rose for my benefit. Not only did it rise, but was faithful to the order of Creation and painted the sky for me. And the Moon would not be left out. The tide of both pulled me from the depths of despair to set my feet upon high places.

Regardless of his shortcomings, Mozart's gift to us has survived centuries. For it is art. It is creative. It is in harmony with the Sun and Moon. Age to age, the message remains sure. Truth is not confined within our limitations.

For the Earth is the Lord's, and the fullness thereof; the world, and they that dwell therein. Lift up your heads, O ye gates; and be ye lift up, ye everlasting doors; and the King of glory shall come in!

Virtue

November 7, 1997

Are you familiar with the female model described in the book of Proverbs, chapter 31, verses 10–31? As you can guess, she's not the prototype of our contemporary bone thin, very rich super-model.

The Proverbial beauty is virtue. The text characterizes the virtuous woman as a trustworthy wife. She's thrifty, a gifted seamstress and an ambitious woman. Conscientious with her household, she rises before dawn to prepare breakfast. Honor and wisdom are her strength graced with generosity.

Granted, these noble standards require large portions of self-sacrifice, especially hospitality. We may consider these values archaic, altering them with a tinge of scorn for our modern lifestyles. (Hot breakfasts fell by the way-side when our girls entered high school.)

Nonetheless, current models of virtue can be found peppered throughout our world. There's one in Newport, Kentucky.

It is my pleasure to introduce you to Pauline. She embraces and maintains the quality of hospitality with a flair. Her home is a Cincinnati *bookend* house that she and her husband, Dennis, restored.

He is an artist with the paintbrush, as she is with the sewing machine. Their talents blend in a unique swirl to produce a gallery of every room in their enchanting three-story masterpiece.

Pauline and Dennis make you feel warmly welcome and pampered beyond justification when within their tall walls. Pauline's kindness gives charm to their antique furniture and talking wood floors. Security dwells richly in every room.

The two are foster parents. This satisfies Pauline's outreach to the needy as well as provides a companion for

Matthew, their five-year-old son. They presently foster a darling four-year-old named Rebecca.

Rebecca is one of three children victimized by an abusive father. The young mother took action upon discovery of the violence and removed her children from the home for their protection.

Pauline's virtue oozed from her as she described the child's good nature. Her heart breaks for the mother and child. She can't imagine losing her "Matty." She can't imagine her Matty losing her.

One morning, she was on the stairs leading down to the kitchen when she heard Matty and Rebecca talking. They were just chatting away, waiting for Pauline to make their breakfast. She told me how wonderfully strange it was to hear two voices coming from the kitchen. (It had been some time since another child had been in their home.) She paused to listen to the joyful conversation—so grateful for sweet Rebecca.

As the three sat at breakfast, Rebecca announced to Pauline that she needed to snuggle. Pauline gladly lifted the girl upon her lap, giving affirmations of love and acceptance.

Matty was not to be overlooked and responded, "I need some snuggling too."

Pauline's wisdom promised Matty many snuggles when Rebecca was finished with hers (Pauline nor Rebecca were in any hurry).

Without any prompting from Pauline, Rebecca scooted over to one leg and told Matty with confidence, "You can snuggle too, Matty. There is room for two childs."

Pauline responded in awe that the little victim on her lap could so generously share what she so desperately needed. Matty was in his mother's lap in a wink, and for some of the sweetest moments in her life, Pauline snuggled her two "childs."

Yes, Pauline knows how to season the sad places of broken hearts with pure love and hospitality. How she can embrace these little ones, then release them to uncertain circumstances is beyond me. Her strength and maturity are rare and admirable.

Our society has allowed the needy to fall between the cracks, leaving them to government programs. I'm guilty too.

But in Newport, Kentucky, a mother's arms reach outside of her home to draw a little child into safety for a season. She takes time out of her busy day to touch with her healing hands and words.

Pauline people encourage us to rethink how we can better serve the needy: to find our style of servanthood. They remind us that virtue is found in the lap of a loving man or woman, the safest place in the world for a child.

Sweet Shakespeare

November 19, 1997

Recently I attended a meeting that included the November threnody, "Autumn Leaves," as a part of the meeting's program. The song's melancholy tune and woeful words gently vexed my otherwise contented heart. Summer's colorful death has always brought me bittersweet feelings. The light leaves fall heavy on the earth, bringing tremors in the transfer of seasons.

The piano keys playing "Autumn Leaves" also strummed the memory of a special November birthday … my Becky's. Her dad's little Mustang drove her home from the hospital twenty-seven years ago on a clear, crisp Thanksgiving eve, held adoringly in my arms. It was my first Thanksgiving as a mother. Becky was a delightful distraction from foreboding falling leaves.

I related to the songwriter's lamenting lyrics, "but I miss you most of all, my darling, when autumn leaves start to fall." They reminded me that I couldn't touch Becky's "sun-tanned hand" on her birthday. She is dead. A season once anticipated and celebrated now offers rueful reminders.

I half heard the words, floating between composure and memory. Becky's last holiday with us was two Thanksgivings ago. We celebrated her twenty-fifth birthday the next day.

My meditations ended with the song. I thought I had everything under control as I rose from my seat and drove home. But the emotion rubbed death's deep wound. I was bleeding internally again, unaware. The following days were teary and filled with internal conflict.

In the privacy of my quiet place, healing words found me in my distress. I opened a letter (sealed with medical tape) from my sister Sonia and her husband, Brent. These very busy young parents (of four children) took time to encourage me from their heart. Sonia's poem invited me to dance again. Brent shared with me from his journal.

And guess what he wrote about? "November is the month of leaf fall." Oh, yes, I heard the message. "And November winds use the bare twigs as the strings of a harp to make a song of lamentation … as the strings of a harp on which to make a November threnody. Of the leaves we say, 'After life's fitful fever they sleep well.'" (William A. Quale) It was like reading a gentle Shakespeare.

But of course! Brent loves Shakespeare. His passion for literature inspires and teaches me of its beauty and grace.

Some days after receiving his medicinal words, I spoke with Brent during a phone call. "Thanks, Shakespeare, for the eloquent words of encouragement from your journal."

"Oh, I didn't write the journal text." Brent explained the journal reference in his letter is a devotional, written by numerous authors, not himself. He was flattered I considered him capable of the writing and apologized for the misunderstanding.

But there was no misunderstanding. Brent was indeed the bearer of language and beauty. He took a few minutes in a quiet morning and spent them with me. He transformed a song of lamentation into a lullaby.

Ahhh … wonderful words. As they wounded, so they healed. The autumn leaves fell softly in sweet encouragement and now lay still, giving rest to a fitful soul.

Mom's Turkey Roaster

November 26, 1997

This is the time of year the strong pull of blood gathers Americans from Earth's four-corners to sit around a table set with a golden brown turkey. An inherent lasso draws hearts in pilgrimage to observe *Thanksgiving Day.*

Tradition. What would we do without it? I'm convinced we would self-destruct by our own ambitions if we didn't have this built-in safety valve. A mechanism that takes us back to family, warmed by the heat of the oven. A house filled with flavors of steaming mashed potatoes, dressing, and candied yams. And plenteous pies with real whipped cream.

Thank God for tradition. It invades our memory to recall certain markers in our lives we overlooked as children. Lasting memorials to past times that grow richer with age ... like a fine wine. Something to connect us to what was once our reality, lest we forget to taste the sweetness in a sometimes bitter world.

It's strange, but I hardly remember Mom's delicious turkeys. I remember the mammoth turkey roaster as she pulled it out of the oven. How Mom turned her face from the heat, lifting her tasty burden, a prize for anxious and hungry guests. Once the turkey was carved and consumed, Mom placed the wishbone on the stove. (Years later, upon my query, she told me she put it there "to dry out.")

That's when the turkey roaster took on the role I remember most. A Saturday soon after Thanksgiving, Mom filled the turkey roaster with homemade decorated sugar cookies. My favorite was (and remains) the wreath, bearing cinnamon candy berries.

She stored the sweet container in the bottom cupboard for easy access. She must have become very familiar with the sound of hungry hands lifting the lid and searching for a favorite. I recall the goodies almost lasting until Christmas, even with five munching daughters in the house.

My tradition was to recline in my favorite chair, legs dangling over one arm and head resting on the other, and nibble tiny cookie pieces until it disappeared. Yes, my mother is clearly responsible for my sweet tooth.

And she is responsible for developing tradition within my human spirit. She was the heart of our home. As most mothers, she did not receive the applause she deserved. Human thankfulness is slow to develop. Thank God she has survived to receive honor from a finally thankful daughter!

Dear reader, let's be careful to sit among fellow pilgrims, where we find strength to stand in adversity. May we as Americans always gather together to celebrate the past and give a good tug on Future's wishbone.

Yes, thank God for tradition … for ancestral muscles that hold our disjointed members together, so we can pull a turkey apart.

A Favorite

December 24, 1997

One of the criteria to make a child's story a classic is the application it makes to the adult. This is what endears me to such stories as *The Velveteen Rabbit, Peter Pan* and *A Wrinkle in Time*. The message within these books transcends time, soars over oceans and builds bridges between generations.

These stories ripen with age, ever bearing fruit for the hungering sojourner. *The Velveteen Rabbit* ever gives its reader an invitation to become *Real*.

Just how does one become *Real*? By being loved.

You see, the Velveteen Rabbit was a Christmas gift to a young boy who promptly neglected him, as he did most of his toys in the nursery. Sound familiar? This much has not changed since Margery Williams wrote the book in 1922.

If the English Ms. Williams were alive today, I would love to have a chat with her over a pot of tea. We would discuss how the Rabbit grappled with the waiting to be loved and then the discomfort love brought him. I would put myself in the Rabbit's velvet skin and ask the author as the Rabbit did the Skin Horse, who was both wise and *Real*, "What is *REAL*?"

"Real isn't how you are made," she would reply as did the Skin Horse. "It's a thing that happens to you. When a child loves you for a long, long time, not just to play with, but REALLY loves you, then you become Real. It doesn't happen all at once. You become. It takes a long time. Generally, by the time you are Real, most of your hair has been loved off, and your eyes drop out and you get loose in your joints and very shabby. But these things don't matter at all, because once you are Real you can't be ugly, except to people who don't understand."

And I, like the Rabbit, would wrestle with the part about becoming *Real* taking a long, long time … and becoming shabby. Why? Because they are hurtful happenings.

But the story continues, and the boy loved the Rabbit. In the transformation, the Rabbit didn't even notice his whiskers were pulled out and his velvet was worn off. The Rabbit became *Real* to the boy. And when he was later separated from the boy, anxious times caused him to ask, "Of what use was it to be loved and lose one's beauty and become Real if it all ended like this?" His sorrow produced a tear that ran down his shabby nose.

As nursery magic goes, when the tear fell to the ground, a flower grew with a Fairy enfolded. She changed him into a Real Rabbit that could dance with the other rabbits. He was at home with the other rabbits in Rabbitland where he lived for ever and ever.

The Velveteen Rabbit is as Real to me as my own set of circumstances. That is why I go to his story when I feel like I don't fit anywhere … when love's rub hurts. The simple story speaks to the child within me. It reminds me I am a human *being*, and am always in the process of *becoming*.

So when life becomes so very complicated and hurtful, which is it more likely to do around Christmastime, the Velveteen Rabbit hops into my heart and invites me to become *Real*. He does his funny little dance before me, reminding me God has loved me from the beginning, and He will always love me.

Isn't that the message of Christmas? If we truly believe in Christmas, we know Christ has the power to make us Real.

Yes, *The Velveteen Rabbit* speaks to our lives like a sweet parable, giving us hope for love — and for our Real home. You see, Love doesn't end like this, it lives in a place where we will dance for ever and ever.

Uncle Herm

December 31, 1997

His name is Herman Glen McCoy, and I would know the sound of his steps and voice anywhere. Mom also knew his inimitably sure and slow gait when he entered the back door of her house, and said so before seeing him.

"That's Herm!" she predicted. Mom and I were relaxing in her pair of "lazy-girl" chairs when his familiar frame passed through the kitchen doorway. The position of my chair gave me first view of my uncle. Mom smiled with silent, warm delight at the sound of his voice. He had taken the easy stroll from his house to Mom's for a Christmas visit.

It was more than good to see him. "Where's Aunt Dean?" I asked, for my aunt and uncle are usually inseparable.

"She's up visiting with her mother," he explained, pulling a kitchen chair away from the table to join us in the family room. I asked how my great-aunt Hazel was doing.

"Fine," he replied.

He would not accept any offers for dessert, saying he was "full as a tick." We all laughed in response, his eyes disappearing into dark slits above his high cheekbones with only a gleam visible. I studied the lines in my uncle's strong face, remembering his laughing eyes from my childhood.

Staying in the moment, I envisioned my risky ride on the handlebars of Uncle Herm's bicycle when I was a toddler. Mom has told me the story a thousand times as she laughs, confessing how she feared for the life of her baby in the hands of her carefree brother. But I survived for him to laugh at my childish insistence that his chickens were crowing "Uncle Hermy!" and had four legs. He was my Uncle Hermy until I had children.

Uncle Herm and Aunt Dean always had time to sit with their nieces and nephews and join their fun. Once Uncle Herm sat with stocking feet resting on his coffee table, pretending to use sign language with my deaf cousin, Kevin, making up his hand motions as he went along. We all laughed so hard. But Uncle Herm's eyes laughed the most. He had no less time for his grandnieces/nephews. The most hilarious event was the evening he gave each niece and nephew a $20 bill for standing on their head — in the same room where we presently sat. He shelled out a lot of money that night!

But there's no deeper impression than his laughter as he tells the story about our encounter with a "wasper's" nest during blackberry picking one summer. That's when I learned about ticks by my own skin. But the blackberry cobbler and jam were well worth the hazards.

Mom interrupted my moment of meditation by asking, "Doesn't Herm look sharp?"

Like you see in the movies, my mind adjusted the haze of memory to focus closely on my uncle. I saw him with different eyes as I studied his strong hands on his thick thighs. His broad shoulders and gentle eyes once again nurtured me as they have all my life.

What a paradox. A simple man of the earth, yet my hero — a king, a savior. My meek Uncle Herm has inherited the earth of my heart. And I in turn have inherited his love for simplicity, solitude and nature. How blessed is my human soul to sit in the company of this humble man and catch the beam of light from his eyes. Even more so, how blessed I am to have his steps embedded in the soil of my soul.

Seize the Day

January 7, 1998

Browsing through Borders Books for a birthday card, I stumbled upon a writer's delight. Famous faces were featured on a card with a quote and their signature. I selected several cards to take home because their words captured life unique to the writer. Did these great minds, such as Albert Einstein and Emily Brontë, did they know their words would be preserved to influence future hungry minds?

Jane Austen's quote is the most pleasantly puzzling to me. "*Why not seize the pleasure at once? How often is happiness destroyed by preparation, foolish preparation.*" To me, her writing, her characters within her novels (*Pride and Prejudice*) do not portray impulsive pleasure seekers. Her female heroines are usually conservative patient women who wait with self-control and integrity for their true love. Just what does she mean by "seizing pleasure?"

I would hazard a guess Ms. Austen wrote this statement toward the end of her short life. Chances are she reached the vantage point to see both sides of life, and the view gave her inspiration to speak her mind in saying *carpe diem*. Enjoying the pleasure of the moment is a childhood ability we lose as we learn responsibility and the benefits of planning, be it short or long range goals. We usually don't return to spontaneity until grandchildren come along or we face a life-threatening circumstance that shocks us into living the life before us.

Seizing the pleasure at once means leaving my kitchen duties to join the three little women next door when they use my hillside for a snowy time of fun. I didn't seize that wintry night three weeks ago. Will it ever return for my enjoyment? I was too busy preparing for something else. I can't even remember what it was.

Yes, my point of view is changing. This is one advantage to being over the hill. Life looks different on the other side. Preparation has its place, and it is not before spontaneity. How many times have our carefully detailed plans been foiled? Do we throw ourselves into fits of anger and discouragement, or do we seize the alternate opportunity at hand? We can't even see the other option because of our *foolish preparation*!

I am by no means advocating we cast aside goals and plans. They are a necessary function of successful living. But plans perish for lack of dreams and visions. And we cannot plan our dreams. They arrive unannounced, just like most marvelous opportunities.

Welcome your dreams. Make room for them. Take them up. Embrace them. Play with them like a child.

Day by day, allow inspiration to visit you and return you to the happiness of living in the moment. Days will turn into weeks, weeks into months, and before you realize it, a year of creative living will have been yours.

So, dear reader, what is *your* great mind dreaming of this new year? I encourage you to let the dream take you places you've never been before. Plunge into its stream and seize the pleasure. Drink of today's life. It is a happiness not to be destroyed.

Presents and Pirates

January 14, 1998

If I could have any gift of my choice, of anything in this entire world, it would be the locket my mother gave me back in the early eighties. I loved the round, gold piece the moment I laid my eyes upon it.

Mom's face was glowing as the gold itself, hinting at the contents of the box when she handed me the gift. I knew the gift was special from the look on her face.

The locket was about an inch and a half in diameter and hung on a gold chain. It was elegant, yet was of good weight—sort of like my relationship with my mother— beautiful, yet strong and sturdy. A delicate design was engraved in the gold, giving it an antique attitude.

I opened the locket to find a miniature portrait of my mother in one side, her gray hair shining in contrast to her dark pink dress. My hand took it to my heart in breathless joy and appreciation. I knew I had been given a keepsake— an heirloom. How marvelous, how intimate a gift! One I cherished immediately.

And when my days on Earth would come to an end, the locket would be passed on to my eldest daughter, with my picture facing my mother on the other side. And when my daughter no longer lived to wear it, she would pass it on to her daughter … and so it goes with such treasures.

Yes, I wore the locket with great honor and pride for several years. The value of the locket grew every time I slipped it over my head. The treasure penetrated my heart, becoming a part of me.

Then one day, thieves broke into our house and greedily took my precious gift without conscience or thought for my kind mother and me. They also stole other treasures, the few we had, throwing family possessions in crazed fashion throughout the house. Stunned, I staggered from room to room in disbelief, violence tearing my treasures from me. How could human beings deal so cruelly with another? To trade treasures given and accepted by pure hearts for evil intentions!

Over a decade has passed since the plunder of my home. I sometimes wonder, "Where in the world is my locket?" Has it landed around someone else's neck? Did it fall into a sewer as the thieves ran from a pursuer? Just where is my treasure?

I rather fancy my gold locket has found its home in the kingdom of lost and stolen treasures. A *Treasure Island*, if you will. For our world has always had pirates who have no regard for the honest and honorable giving and receiving of gifts. They don't understand you can't steal the significance of a treasure. You can't touch it with human hands.

A treasure's value is held in the heart, fully infused within the human spirit. Yes, real treasures are not of this world, where thieves break in and steal. The true treasure dwells in the chest of love. And there my gold locket is, safe from the pirate's pillage.

The Stream of Consciousness

February 20, 1998

You'll have to forgive me, dear reader, for I have mixed musings swarming in my mind today. I'm silly from studying and trying to figure out the complicated issues of life. My country walk is the only thing that seems to make sense to me today. Theories and analyses can't restore my human soul. I came dangerously close to forgetting to return to the fresh sameness of eons.

My neighbors who own the old farm on the corner were outside, piling up firewood. Steve operated the chainsaw while Katie split the logs. I admired Katie for her strength. The way she lifted the ax with little effort, and "Whack!" the log fell to the ground. She picked up the log, threw it on the pile and then, "Whack!" again. I'm such a wimp. There's no way I could do that without some serious upper-body conditioning.

The young farmers enjoy good, hard work. At day's end, they sometimes sit in soothing silence on their back-yard porch. They rock themselves in comfort of the shelter they have made for each other and their little girl. What more could a person want?

And what would a country walk be without barking dogs? Another farm on my route has a mixture of old yellow and black labs and miscellaneous mutts. The leader of the pack is an old, shabby thing who sounds downright pitiful when he barks. He's way past laryngitis. I feel sorry for the old fella. I almost feel guilty making him bark.

Lo and behold, if a wolf-like dog didn't start barking up my back as I turned my first corner! What's up with these dogs today, I thought. I stopped to make friends with him, but he persisted in his barking, refusing my friendship. Okay, be that way. I continued my walk and within ten minutes managed to irritate another dog or two. They ran around their yard like I was some criminal ready to kick down their front door. Why do dogs do this barking thing, anyway? By this point, I had rethought my thoughts about possibly doing the pet thing again. How could I adjust to all this obsessive barking? Is there such a thing as doggie Ritalin?

Finally, I reached a quiet place. I stopped to listen to the slow winter water flow under the one-lane bridge. Oh, to be at such ease. No hurry. Just rolling along. I straddled and sat on the road barricade, looking into the dark bottom of the stream. The moving mirror gave my reflection. I watched the water continually pass under the bridge. Where does this stream come from? Where does it go? It just keeps passing and passing under the bridge. I spit into the water and watched the tiny drop float away from me. I wished every troubled soul could find such a sacred place. I spit again.

My eyes lifted to the new development that is tearing at the edges of my country paradise. They had better not destroy my wild raspberries, trillium and wild iris! Peace was disturbed by resentment and another barking dog. Serenity passed.

Turning my last corner where good ol' Sparky always hung out, I thought how *he* never barked. He was *the* most contented dog. He was completely loveable. But he passed away last year. Now, if I could find a dog like Sparky.

My walk is done and I've returned to my computer. Sure enough, everything passes. But there is no reason for lamentation. For this season shall pass also. Midterms are this week, then—San Francisco, here I come! I'll enjoy each passing day of Spring Break as Kelly and I flow in the stream of life and loving. Then, I'll return home to work, school and my computer. Oh, how beautiful. The flow of life continues.

Holes in the Clouds

March 4, 1998

My plane landed with the rain on the San Francisco runway. But the downpour didn't dampen my excitement. All I could think about was retrieving my luggage and making my way outside to find Kelly by the curb. Eight days of vacation were waiting for my daughter and me.

The airport smacked with the scent of a tropical climate. Ah … palm trees, flowers, green grass and sunglasses. Yes, my sunglasses were packed in faith. It just *couldn't* rain for eight straight days!

Kelly broke the hypnotic spell the baggage conveyor cast upon me. Dressed in her fisherman's knit sweater, she was a sight for sore eyes. After hugs and loading up luggage, she led us into an adventure of a lifetime.

We stopped by Office Depot on our way home to her apartment. The Asian San Franciscans created a scene that resembled one wet visit several years ago in Hong Kong. The masses of dark heads under umbrellas made me forget for a moment that I was in the United States. The diversity of California was drawing me into its unique charm.

We took umbrellas and raincoats that evening to navigate the wet roads and sidewalks to the San Francisco Symphony. Kelly began our vacation with a musical surprise for my birthday! Jetlag closed my eyes a few times during the performance, but not a measure of music was missed. The rain ended with the concert, and we walked into a delightful evening of café hunting. (If Kelly weren't embarrassed easily by her mother's bragging, I would digress here a bit to tell you how quickly she has discovered her new city's enclaves. And respecting her wishes, I won't elaborate on her patience with me when I ran red lights and frightened pedestrians who fled from a crazy Michigan driver. By some miracle, we always made our destination on time, without a fatality.)

We enjoyed cappuccino in ambiance tastier than our beverage. The following day the sky cleared and we toured Victorian homes. We strolled streets dense with one-of-a-kind shops. We chased the sunshine from turn to turn and found a hill to climb to view the sun's disappearance and the Bay's glittering twilight. Oh yes, glorious *summum bonum* of life. A Wordsworth "spot of time," high and lifted up above the cares of the world.

The following days were no less full of exquisite moments. A drive south on Highway 1 took us to Santa Cruz, Carmel and Monterey. We continued to chase the holes in the clouds and watched the ocean waves explode against the battered shoreline. The sun shined on the yellow bloom of wild clover, covering the emerald green grass. Everywhere our eyes could see, there was Beauty. Flowers bloomed in every crag and crevice. Oh, the glory of wild California Poppies!

The sun continued to shine on the Napa and Sonoma valleys, Golden Gate Park, Redwood forests and the walruses at Fisherman's Wharf. How comical those barking sea-creatures were! They lay sunbathing on several large wooden platforms in the Bay … just like one big, happy family. These sun-worshippers lifted their whiskery noses toward the sky and enjoyed the warmth. All of us humans just had to laugh.

Friends joined us in an English teahouse for our last evening in Tony Bennett's *City by the Bay.* We talked and laughed about our dreams, and how we will use our gifts to make these dreams come true.

The next morning brought farewells to family and friends and later my plane landed with the rain on a Detroit Metro runway. But the clouds did not discourage me. Bright memories shined through. They warmed my heart as I lifted my face to see their rays through the holes in the clouds.

Kindness or Consequences

March 11, 1998

Asking a silent blessing over my Wendy's junior cheese-burger, I thought of *Visine* again. Taking my first bite, I wondered if I would ever be rid of this word when I ordered or opened my gourmet drive-thru bag. And will I ever fully forget the mental picture of the cook stamping on a steak when I walk into a restaurant to enjoy a fine meal? I know I know ... you're shaking your head and asking yourself, "What on earth is Iris talking about?"

Honestly, I have a perfectly logical explanation for your query. And even though I am mostly sane and sensible, I wonder if I should enlighten you on the subject, for you may suffer the same haunt as I. Nonetheless, the proverbial limb is tempting me, so here goes.

Warning! Proceed with caution.

In one of my Communications classes one evening, the subject of our responses to people in public and our attitude motivating those responses was discussed. The class divided into our small groups to share our individual responses to difficult situations and people. We were to focus on the dominating attitude behind our response. Sounds harmless, doesn't it?

Never underestimate the creativity of the young adult. Responses were rather typical until one young man who happens to bartend told the class about his remedy for a demanding customer. He explained that the public is mistaken to think they are in control and that the "customer is always right." Furthermore, if a bartender doesn't like a customer, "all it takes is a few drops of Visine in his drink, and he's in the bathroom for a few days."

The entire class, professor included, gasped spontaneously to such extreme behavior. The true confession of the drastic measure instigated another restaurant story. I sat in amazement at the ease in which these young people shared their angry vindictiveness with their classmates. It was so *Geraldo-ish.*

A young woman who happens to bartend and hostess proceeded to tell a story about a man who demanded the cook prepare his steak the way *he* wanted it, which was not offered on the menu. The cook finally agreed, after the customer harassed the waitress for several minutes, causing a scene in the restaurant.

The cook took the steak, threw it on the floor, stamped on it and threw on the griddle. He prepared the sauce per customer's instructions, poured the sauce over the steak and threw the steak on the floor again. Covering the steak once again with the sauce, it was served to the customer who ate every bite while the restaurant staff had the last laugh. "We have our ways of getting even," the young servants boasted in agreement.

Pretty scary stuff, isn't it? Can you imagine the implications of such retaliations? Someone could really get hurt. I walked out of the classroom absolutely incredulous that our young people could be so cruel.

Later I was told this kind of vengeance is as old as soup. *Spit in the Soup* is an old, true story about a black man who worked in a kitchen with a white cook. The black man witnessed the cook habitually spit into the soup when he prepared it. Naturally, no one would have believed the black man if he had dared tell. The cook would have denied it anyway, and the black man would probably have been beaten for lying and lost his job.

Now do you understand what encourages my prayer over my burger? Isn't it amazing what one learns in the classrooms of higher education? I've learned that when I order a drink or meal from imperfect strangers, it behooves us to be one kind person.

A Sunny South Window

March 18, 1998

Ahhh … the warmth of the sun on my face and feet. Yes, beware of the ides of March. Sit and meditate upon the blue sky—observe the hint of stubborn green under the blah winter grass.

My sunny south windows coax me to curl up like a lazy cat and enjoy. The wide dining room window is my favorite. Sometimes I lie on the floor in the bright spot on the carpet and pretend the floor is Tahitian sand. My best naps and mini-vacations are taken in those sunspots.

But my most common posture is sitting in a chair with my feet propped up on the window seat. I have watched nine years of seasons turn, turn, turn … all from my sunny south window. Today marked my tenth spring watch.

My window is like a *time machine*. The seasons and years pass on the other side of the glass, changing as quickly as the mannequin in the dress shop window in the movie classic, *The Time Machine*.

I have watched the hawks glide in high prey and caught quick glimpses of the sly fox dart across the yard to disappear in the tall grass. And I watched a house appear in the open field. A few seasons later, another house went up by the edge of the woods. My eyes have seen the white tail of the deer gracefully bound toward their forest den. The faithful sun and moon have arched thousands of times over my window, and rainbows have spanned from east to west. I have seen the morning mist move up the hills and the dew melt into diamonds on blades of grass.

And the same window view told me today of more change. It's not the first time I've had to face the fact that my quiet backyard place, a hidden terrace lined with irises, will not be the same this spring and summer. For there will be no hiding from the house under construction to my west. I must confess I don't feel comfortable about it. The house is pointy and unfriendly. It looks like it could impale a bird in flight.

Yes, my country scene is changing. Writing down my doubts and dreams, I long to capture today, to make time stand still so I don't have to make another decision for the future. To think only of the feeling of the heat on my feet.

Today I found my Sabbath rest where time cannot touch me. Let life change. Let me change. I will watch the passing seasons without fear. I will submit to the change time brings to my mind, soul, spirit and body. And for those times when change turns my stomach with fear, I'll return to my window for rest and remember *this too shall pass.*

Dear friend, I encourage you to linger long in sunny windows … obey the bidding to be aware of the hope that lies within the thawing earth. When the sun is high in the sky, curl up and dream your dreams or sit and watch the ground turn green. Allow the Light to melt winter away as you celebrate the changing season.

A Band of Women

April 1, 1998

Sometimes we humans meet with circles of our kind who are unusually attractive. No, it's not glamour or fame, but a gentle wisdom that invites us into their company. We sense something special and draw near. Before we know it, we are face to face with new friends and mentors.

St. Patrick's Day Eve Julie opened her Farmington residence to her women's group and me. Her festive home served Bailey's Irish cream and various other refreshments to her guests. When I arrived, the family room was lined with middle-aged women who were discussing the recipient of a charitable contribution. Then they presented their prayer requests. I felt like I was on holy ground as they interceded for the needy. And imagine my Protestant surprise when they prayed the rosary. Never before had I been included within such Catholic ranks and rituals.

The women were obviously old friends. They were very comfortable with each other and spoke with great ease as they expressed their opinions and petitions freely. I sat as a silent observer, feeling honored to have the opportunity to present my journal writing experiences to them.

Even though Julie was the only person I had previously met, I didn't feel like a stranger. They warmly accepted me as I stood at one end of the oval human band. We laughed and cried together during the hour and a half of my presentation. The strength of their relationships became very apparent as we disclosed personal sufferings and triumphs. I drew from their strength as the band stretched to include me as a confidant and friend.

After the group wrote a journal entry, I gave them opportunity to read what they had written. To my surprise, no one volunteered at first. Then I realized the special dynamic of this group … they are intimate friends. I asked if they felt intimidated to disclose their entries to their friends. Some nodded yes, but one very outspoken member said, "No, it's just that we all know what the other wrote, so what's the sense in reading it?" Laughter erupted and broke the ice.

The reading began. Again, more tears and laughter as we heard about one woman's adjustment to life since her husband's death and another's shift into retirement. The band became stronger with each reading.

The women have been meeting for over twenty years. They represent a Catholic parish but have become ecumenical with a few "token" Protestants (as their outspoken-spokesperson told me). They have raised their children together and are now watching grandchildren enter their families. They recently buried a member who died of cancer. And they walked through the valley of divorce with a member.

The Farmington women have discovered the bond of sisterhood. They know the power of encouragement and prayer, and they use it with great conviction and skill. It is such bands that hold families together. It is such bands that hold our broken culture together.

Please take courage, dear sister, next time you are attracted to the quiet meekness of sisterhood. There is great strength in a band of women. Join the ranks and feel the gentle pull of intercession. I promise the band will help hold you together through hardships and happiness in life-long relationships.

Sanctuaries

May 15, 1998

Twenty-seven years ago Mother's Day meant diapers timed to go messy just before we walked out the door for church ... then spit-up down my neck in the church nursery. I needed to take a change of clothes for myself as well as the baby! Seldom did I see the inside of the sanctuary. Later, when I did clear the nursery barricade and made it to the adult service, there was no peace from those toddler questions without answers.

Mother's Day dinner in a restaurant grew increasingly impossible with each daughter addition. One year I permitted my baby Ruth to consume an entire dish filled with pats of butter. It kept her quiet. Desperate situations call for drastic measures. Almost anything to finish a meal before it turned stone stiff and cold!

Those hectic, unpredictable days are now memories, mere reflections of darling little girls in lacy socks, black patent shoes and matching home-sewn dresses. Adolescence, teenage and adulthood have all visited my three daughters. Becky died twenty-one months ago, and Kelly lives in San Francisco. Ruth alone remains at home to celebrate my day.

Today, the meaning of Mother's Day is in a state of flux. Redefinition. What am I to expect? To desire? My life has changed. Now I must change.

I thought of this late last night as I waited to hear the relieving sound of Ruth's entrance through the kitchen door. All I desired was time alone with my daughter — if just for an hour. Time to share our hearts with each other. To find a quiet place and listen to each other and God.

Seven Ponds Nature Center in Dryden came to mind. I've heard of it many times but have never taken the time for a visit. Yes, that's where I wanted to spend Mother's

Day morning. In Nature's sanctuary. I hoped Ruth would agree.

She made it home safely. We both slept soundly. After morning broke, I crawled into her bed against her protesting groan to give her my unconventional idea. She was in favor, but only if I gave her another hour to sleep.

I could do that.

For an hour and a half our feet tracked trails filled with jack-in-the-pulpit, Mayapples, wild geraniums, ferns and fenced-in trillium. Birds serenaded us with their canticle of praise as we wandered woods and boardwalks. My Canon shot serene settings Nature presented.

The winding paths led us to a wooden platform where Ruth and I perched to read and meditate on the Psalms. On the edge of a pond, surrounded by tranquility, we communed with each other and God. We risked intimate words we had never uttered before.

Ruth wrote me a gift from her heart and read it to me as we walked the paths toward the parking lot. Her confessions and convictions were held hallowed in our sanctuary. Holiness and righteousness had removed us far from the messes in our lives. At the edge of the woods I sensed we were re-entering the brutal and destructive world. But there was no resisting the passage.

For the first time I knew in my heart my children may leave me, but they will never forget me. My children shall always be under the shadow of my wing. Time and space cannot separate them from their ever present and safe sanctuary—that hallowed place where two hearts touch and commune with one another in holy intimacy.

The Scents of the Season

May 22, 1998

Every season has its peculiar scents. Spring and summer explode with scents such as morning dew, freshly mown grass, wormy rains, dusty roads, sweaty skin, lake-water hair and blossoms of every kind imaginable.

There is an indescribable summer scent wafting in my window … a pervasive scent that greets me when I walk out my door. This spicy fragrance follows me on country walks and clings close to me when I return home.

Just what is producing this bittersweet scent?

I must cause passers-by to question my sanity as I sniff the flowering plants along my roadside route. Like a dog, I go from plant to tree, tree to bush, looking for the source of this most incredible smell. As long as I don't lift my leg, I suppose it's okay to continue my search.

I laugh in spite of myself as my nose inspects the blossom of another disappointment. Will I ever find *the* bloom? Why is it so evasive? I keep sniffing … I keep looking. Maybe someday I'll find the source of the scent. Perhaps it isn't even a flower. Could I be looking in all the wrong places?

The more I think about this invisible pleasure, I realize it is the scent of the present season. A mixture of hidden and visible elements makes it what it is. It is where I am.

Some seasons are purely sweet and palatable. I crave their pleasure. Others smell offensive and are bitter … I want to spit them out of my mouth. Some seasons are bland and without remarkable fragrance or flavor. I can take them or leave them. They pass without my notice.

Then comes the bittersweet season. Its fragrance is alluring, but beyond my understanding and embrace. I can't quite find its source … what purpose it presents to me. I have an idea, but I can't see it and define it. And I am uncomfortable with the unknown.

I can't decide if the scent is desirable or not. It is rich, to be sure, but pungent. Yet there is a sweetness to the fragrance unlike any other.

Oh, these ambiguous seasons! Why can't they pass over me and visit someone else?

No. They ride the breezes through my screened windows and say, "You must take the bitter with the sweet. Sometimes they are inseparable. The mysterious, bittersweet scents are the loveliest of all. They may be bitter in your mouth, but they are sweet to the other senses. They are like a medicine for your wounded soul."

Yes, dear reader, the balance of the bittersweet is to be desired. As we linger among the summer scents, the bitter and the sweet blend to prepare for us the most delicious flavor.

Open the window of your heart to the bittersweet season. Don't be afraid … venture out. Seek the source of the scents. Taste and see if it is not good.

Passing May Moods

June 5, 1998

Where has May gone? Seems like just the other day I was writing May at the top of my documents. What a remarkable May it has been!

Gardens are already blooming full force with colorful flowers. Birds are chirping their little hearts out, and lawn mowers have been busy for weeks now. With the exception of an occasional rain (Memorial Weekend), we've had nothing to complain about.

May is also the month of graduation and wedding invitations. There's a stack of them on my desk. I love this time of the year. It's expensive, but I enjoy these social celebrations and rituals.

As a mid-lifer, the wedding invitations are plentiful. It's that season of my life, my peers. How exciting it is to share this occasion with my friends and family!

My niece Kristie is one of the brides-to-be this summer. Two weeks ago, seventy guests "showered" her with best wishes. She was beautiful and enthusiastic. I can't wait for the wedding. Family is coming in from Kentucky and we're going to celebrate. Generations are going to meet on the dance floor to "hustle." Can't you just see it? McCoys and Hatfields dancing together?

Yesterday afternoon I watched the white train of a wedding gown follow a bride to the marriage altar. Observing such a holy occasion caused me to realize our culture's rituals have significance. I don't know where the bridal train originated, but I'm thankful it has survived our modern times. Its beauty and sense of drama adds an element to the wedding ceremony — a mood of presentation to the groom. I think it rather symbolic how the father usually trips over the train after he releases the arm of his daughter for awkward search of his seat.

And what joy it was to see my friends delight in their daughter's marriage. To gather again with them for one of the most important moments in their lives was indeed an honor. I realized afresh these ceremonies are not to be taken lightly. So much emotion, effort and expense are committed to our rituals. They are not empty, meaningless actions, but are full of mood and truth.

Yes, these occasions put me into meditative moods. So many of my daughters' friends are altar-bound. Even Mikey, a friend's youngest son is getting married, the night before Kristie!

Of course I wonder when it will be my turn to be the mother-of-the-bride. This May has made sure I've been reminded considerably often that the love-bug has bitten. Being a hopeless romantic, it doesn't take much to imagine my daughters standing beside their grooms, with their trains filling the aisle.

The matrimonial mood is sure to linger as May passes into June. It encourages my soul to see young people take the mood of love and make a commitment out of it, especially in times when commitment isn't popular.

Furrows, Fields and Fortunes

June 12, 1998

My brain, swollen with a week's worth of data, told me to put the key in the ignition and drive an hour and a half to McMillan's Furniture in Yale. It was Friday night, and if I had my druthers, I'd head for home to curl up in bed with a good book. But I had furniture to buy, and McMillan's was worth the trip and the time.

The solitary drive to Yale gave me time to plan for my San Francisco daughter, Kelly, and her French friend's visit on June 22. That's why the necessary trip to Yale. Marie-Aline needs a place to sleep for a few weeks, then company from Kentucky will be arriving after she leaves for France.

As I drove deeper into the country, the agrarian scene settled my mind. The open spaces of Irish green were an antidote to my irritated neurological pathways. By the time I reached Yale, I was prepared to make more decisions. The small-town store had just what I was looking for, so business was accomplished and I headed south before dark.

Starved, I stopped in Capac to revisit a dairy stand Kelly and I discovered several years ago when we drove to McMillan's (to select her cedar chest). I could not believe five years had passed since Kelly and I ate our cones together at that same spot. Walking to my car with tacos in hand, I noticed an antique shop's sign, "Shadows of the Past." Yes, indeed, this place holds shadows of the past, I thought.

Driving south on Capac Road, the sunset streamed golden beams under a ceiling of clouds, casting a car shadow to my left. The silhouette was detailed, racing along to keep up with me. After I had dropped my taco all over my clothes and finished my mess, I opened my hand to wave at myself. Yes, I could see my fingers. I smiled at my shadow.

Later I spied a farmer walking in a newly plowed furrow. With head down, he kicked the clods of soil, as if meditating. The sunset cast shadows on one side of the furrow, while laying golden ribbons on the opposite. Yes, I thought, how easy to muse in this place. This is the stuff myths are made of. Just tilt the earth a bit and the ribbons of gold dust will flow into a pot at the end.

My mind was renewed as I imagined God's rainbow finger arched over the earth, pointing to the place where humanity finds fortune. "Here!" he said, "Here! In the place where sorrow's blade has broken the soil of your soul will you find the treasure you seek. Only in the furrows are the seeds of faith, hope and love sown. In the valley of the shadow of death is where my Light is the most golden."

I will confess to you, dear reader, these words are not easy for me to hear. I would rather be enchanted than inspired. Inspiration requires a choice. What am I going to do with the seeds planted in the furrows of my soul? How am I to endure past and present shadows?

By setting my mind on the harvest. Is this not what the farmer in the furrows was thinking? Planning for the future? Ah, yes, the fortune is the peace of mind found in the furrows. That is precisely what I found in the fields along Capac Road. And yes, it was well worth the trip.

Small Things

June 19, 1998

Terry left tending her garden to answer my call. Our mutual passion for earth and flowers led our discussion into the realms of unusual June weather and the added garden hours we were enjoying. Terry has created one of the most remarkable landscapes in the Village of Oxford, giving her much experience to offer me.

I knew she was anxious to return to her flowerbeds, but she kindly entertained my questions and complaints about my clay soil and quack grass. It looked rather shabby compared to Terry's Victorian gardens. I sighed with a tinge of envy, wondering if I'll ever cultivate my dream gardens. Slouched in self-pity, I observed a robin yanking a worm out of the sod. I watched the bird's beak tug at the worm repeatedly until it was fully extracted from the earth.

Impressed by the robin's tenacity and the timing of his appearance, I shared with Terry the serendipitous observation. She proceeded to use the robin and the worm as a metaphor of one of life's greatest lessons: it's the small things in life that are the most meaningful.

Terry remarked that it's the small things that hold the big stuff together for her. If she didn't take time to smell the flowers, she wouldn't be who she is. It's the small things, the small, yet profound things of beauty and truth, that add up to make life what it is.

Terry explained that she is all the small things she experiences. She has learned if she doesn't appreciate the small things, she messes up the order of life. She messes up her life and the life of those around her.

"It's the small things that make life worth the effort," she reminded me.

I had to agree, knowing I would not abandon my desire and commitment to cultivate a yard full of blooming flowers. After Terry's encouragement, I was determined not to give up. To me, the small things, like a bouquet of fresh roses, give my life immeasurable value and enjoyment.

Yes. The small things make me who I am.

Terry and the robin remind me to persevere. To keep my beak to the ground. I will eventually have my reward. Gardener and bird teach me the great mysteries and truths of life.

I won't envy Terry's talents or her gardens.

I won't even envy the robin.

Oh, one last small thing. I'm very thankful I'm not the worm.

Singing Anthems

July 1, 1998

Summer is, among many things, a very patriotic time of the year. As I write, firecrackers are hissing in the night air. The evidence of America's mood to celebrate our freedom is everywhere. Flags fly in testimony to our nation's independence from England. A sense of national unity waves in a familiar arrangement of stars and stripes in red, white and blue.

Like most red-blooded Americans, I grew up honoring this American symbol and the lives lost in gaining and protecting our sovereignty. But two weeks ago, the flag took on new meaning.

I watched the Prestonsburg High School gymnasium swell to capacity. Friends and relatives, the likes of my mom, sisters and me, sat in anticipation of the entrance of the 1998 graduating class. We passed Hannah around to pass the time. Hannah is the youngest offspring of the Hatfield-McCoy union, being my darling niece. It was a sight to see aunts and uncles on both sides bounce Hannah on their knee. What else do you do with a cute baby?

I opened the printed program and saw "The National Anthem … Jeremy Ryan Hatfield, Song Leader." This was my nephew's final solo of his high-school career. His life would not be the same from this point of passage. I wondered where the future would find him. Where he would go. What he would do.

Following the processional, a rush went through me when Jeremy was introduced. I placed my hand over my heart for the National Anthem. Being the sap I am, the sight and sound of American masses singing the National Anthem evoked a lump in my throat.

As Jer sang, I quietly joined his lead. The concluding words are a question to the patriot. "Oh, say does the star-spangled banner yet wave, o'er the land of the free and the home of the brave?"

Yes, the presence of the flag brought a sense of security to me. It hung high above Jeremy. It hung high above the Hatfields and McCoys. All it represents drew north to south and south to north. We were united in that place at that time to support Jeremy. We stood in agreement for one young man's success in life. When life gets tough for Jer, he knows he can count on his flesh and blood for love and support.

The Hatfields and McCoys sang an anthem to Jeremy on June 12, 1998. We proclaimed a common commitment. We work, we sacrifice to establish a home for the brave. A home where our children are free to leave because they are sovereign beings.

For generations it has been so, and so it shall be. What a privilege it is to stand and sing an anthem of freedom and courage to our children! How awesome it is to stand in unity under the banner bought by the blood of my forefathers.

That is exactly what the American flag represents to me. Sovereignty and solidarity.

God forbid we take these freedoms lightly and lose them. May we Americans always answer in anthem, "Yes, the star-spangled banner yet waves … o'er the land of the free and the home of the brave."

When Our Best Is Average

July 8, 1998

It is inevitable in one's lifetime to experience personal disappointment when falling short of a goal. There are times when no matter how seriously we apply ourselves to a given task it is simply impossible to realize the desired outcome.

We operate within limitations. We can strive for perfection, but our humanness will emerge as a flaw somewhere on the canvas of our lives. This is reality.

There are times when we know we could perform better, but the demands of life bring compromise to our standard. We have too much on our plates. Something has to give.

Two weeks ago I was wrapping up two classes at Oakland University. My history class was giving me a run for my tuition money. A six-page paper and final exam were due within two days of each other. Working full time, I gave what time I had to both, knowing it wasn't enough to do my best. Compromise was necessary, and a C+ was returned on my paper. Considering my circumstances, average was my best.

In our high performance culture, doing our best has become an expectation. We encourage our children to always "do your best." We strive as adults to give 100% to our employers, family and friends.

But is this possible with the loads we carry? Can we realistically expect ourselves and others to master all things and *be* all things?

Life can impose some severe circumstances upon us. Sickness, death and other tragedies can take the wind out of our sails. It is in these times that getting out of bed in the morning is doing good. Actually, it is the best the bereaved can do. Sometimes simply surviving loss and abuse is doing our best.

Consider the learning disabled. They study and practice their subject with greater effort than the naturally gifted only to earn an average score. In reality, average is their best.

As the rules of golf indicate, we have handicaps. But we are not naturally satisfied with mediocrity. We keep swinging away until we perfect our skills and achieve our goals. This is good. But if we are not careful, we can self-destruct before we learn that being average is sometimes better, healthier, than being best.

Submitting to an average score went against my grain. It is hard for me to accept the fact that it is not humanly possible for me to *be* my best and *do* my best at all times. The truth is, no one can function at such an energy level without taking the joy out of living. I can't always write *A* papers. I'm learning to be content with average results when my average is all I can do.

When our best is average, it is best to take it in stride. Being average isn't so bad after all. It truly does make life more enjoyable, reduces stress and makes us a lot easier to live with.

Building Bridges

July 29, 1998

Last weekend the Underwood household enjoyed controlled chaos. My sisters Patty and Sonia came from out of town with their families to attend our niece's wedding. Four hectic days and hilarious nights were filled with wedding rehearsals, ceremonies, receptions, graduation and birthday parties. We made the most of our opportunities.

A thousand stories passed by my eyes as family members interacted, caught up in moments passing too quickly to capture other than on film. Nieces and nephews filled every floor and bathroom of my house. Garments hung on every available hook in preparation for the wedding (and we all made it to the church on time).

Mom was flapping her feathers at the wedding, surrounded by her fifteen grandchildren. Mike and Kristie tied the knot without a hitch. Then we were off to the reception where Mom's offspring dominated the dance floor until midnight.

Between dances, Hannah, the one and only great-grandchild, entertained our family with her baby charm. Toddling around a chair and showing her five new teeth, she made us laugh and provoked the flash of many cameras.

Victoria (age 7), the former family belle of the ball, participated in our fun with Hannah. I thought how quickly time deposes our little ones from their thrones. Who would someday fill Hannah's little shoes? The brevity of infancy, of childhood, made me wince. I wanted to embrace Victoria and twirl her again to hear her baby giggle. I wished I could stop time—keep Hannah in her little dress with silk flower petals folded inside fine netting—until I was ready to let her grow up.

Hannah and Victoria both spent the night at my home with their parents, with the older surrendering to her successor as graciously as a child can manage. Once Hannah and her parents had left my home for the final gathering of the weekend, Victoria settled into play with her older sister, Erin.

After some good conversation with Victoria's dad and older brother, I went downstairs where my daughter Kelly, Erin and Victoria were sitting on the floor playing with Legos. I asked them what they were doing.

Victoria replied, "Building bridges."

They continued to play without interruption—building their bridges—as I turned to leave.

Victoria is no longer a baby. She is now building bridges with her sister, and Kelly is building with them. How wonderful.

My twenty-three-year-old daughter built a bridge indeed, between seasons in her cousin's lives, from Victoria's solo on center stage to her place on the crowded dance floor.

I guess you could say my family built some serious bridges last weekend. Kristie and Mike built a bridge at the marriage altar. Two families were joined for the first time in history. Now we have the pleasure to support their bridge.

We build bridges by being present, available to help in the time of transition. We can't stop time, growth and change, but we can provide companionship during the journey. Kelly, Erin and Victoria built life bridges.

Dear friend, there is nothing to dread in letting go our childhood as long as we remain as a child within our heart. There will always be opportunities to build bridges with the people we love, especially when there are children and Legos around.

Watching the Corn Grow

August 5, 1998

Watching the corn grow this summer reminded me of the Southern vacations my family enjoyed when I was a child. We made no trips to Disney Land or out west, east or north. My sisters and I knew nothing of life above Grand Blanc, where my mom's geographically closest relatives lived. Saginaw was just a city we had heard about, and the Upper Peninsula seemed like a foreign country. Many of our neighborhood playmates drove north to something called a cottage while the O'Brien family drove to Phelps, Kentucky, to see their *Granny*, not *grandmother*.

My sisters and I were most familiar with boring Ohio, the state with miles and hours of cornfields that separated us from our destination and cousins. There was some fascination, however, in the perfectly planted rows of green cornstalks. The farmers ordered the rows to open for a split second as our car whizzed by, one after another, hypnotizing my childlike mind with their rapid succession. The rhythm entertained me.

This scene unconsciously enhanced my hankering for Granny's home cooking. Through the years, the smell of roastin' ears, garden green beans, and tomatoes became associated with summer. The *garden* was as much a part of my childhood summer as were lazy mornings and late nights with my cousins.

After playing hard all day, a table set with fresh garden vegetables was a welcomed and tasty sight. One of our favorite things to do after our evening bath was to gather at the kitchen table and snack on leftovers … green beans and cornbread. The thought of a mess of beans still makes my mouth water!

To this day my mom uses the strong appeal of garden vegetables upon my taste buds. Predictably, every summer she has lured me to her doorstep with the mention of garden beans and corn. Her bait sounds something like this: "Iris, when are you coming down to visit? The sweet-corn and beans are in. Uncle Herm gave me some beans from his garden, and my white sweet-corn is really good this summer."

Yes, it's that time of the year again. I watched the corn grow along Rochester Road this summer in my travels. I observed the seedlings and the brown soil slowly disappear with the full foliage of dark green stalks. Then, behind my back one weekend, the tassels appeared to surprise me on my Monday drive to work.

The Rochester Road rows are planted parallel to the road, not cracking open like the perpendicular rows for the fun of the passer-by. Nonetheless, I enjoy watching the corn grow. It means I'll soon hear the crunch of sweet-corn once again and taste its sweet flavor, seasoned with butter.

Tomorrow morning, the Rochester stalks will wave their tassels good-bye to my daughters and me as we drive south for the McCoy family reunion. We will feast on Southern cookin' and stories. Stories spun on the spindle of simple things, like the funny things Granny used to say, and tying-up tomatoes with Uncle Tab, and swinging on front porch swings with my cousins … stories about what matters most to us as individuals and family.

Stories about long, boring drives through Ohio that almost drove our mother crazy. About a two-tone, green 1959 Dodge, with fins more suitable for swimming than driving. Stories about driving through miles and miles of cornfields to reach a place Mom called "home"—a table spread with sweet-corn. Corn that not only nourished our bodies, but fed our souls.

Now, I ask you, how could a child possibly be bitter about boring, corny Ohio when corn tastes so sweet? And that, perhaps, is why I enjoy watching the corn grow.

Moving Mantles

August 21, 1998

Mom is moving. Why is this such a hard pill for me to swallow? Because Mom is pulling up McCoy roots to transplant them further south in Florida, leaving the place of my birth and stability.

My sisters and I have seen this coming for several years. None of us wanted Mom to move from her Kentucky home. We want to believe it is best for her. She can't keep up her large house any longer, her gardens and fruit trees. She lives alone and needs convenient and good health care.

The Florida senior communities are tailored for Mom and millions like her. Even though I made the trip to Florida with her to satisfy my need to see her future home for myself, it's hard to imagine Mom's home someplace else.

Among many things, I can't picture Mom's home without her fireplace mantle. My sister Patty put it perfectly during our family reunion a few weekends ago. Mom, Patty and I sat in Mom's family room, enjoying our last morning together in Mom's house. We discussed our past, present and future. Mom verbally listed the items she was leaving behind.

Patty objected to the mention of the coffee table. "Mom, you can't part with your coffee table! All our kids toddled around this table. They cut their teeth on it!"

"But I won't have room for everything in my new house," Mom explained.

Patty silently reflected, looking toward the fireplace mantle. I followed my sister's eyes, in union with her sentiments, yet understanding our mother. "Mom," she spoke tenderly, "you have filled your mantle with your grandkids' pictures."

173

Yes, indeed, sixteen grandchildren have grown-up on Mom's mantle—family faces from cradle to cap and gown—trophies of a life dedicated to family.

We three focused on the most recent graduates displayed on the mantle. "What are you going to do without your mantle, Mom?" I asked, feeling again the sharp jab of loss.

Mom answered honestly that she hadn't thought about it. None of us had.

The mention of mantles led us next door on an expedition to the vacant Homeplace. We were in search of two mantles removed from the farmhouse fireplaces during modernization. We opened the most formidable door of our childhood (we all knew bats lived behind that door!) and climbed the sooty, creaky attic steps. Finding no flying opposition, we resurrected one mantle, staircase post and a wooden ironing board. Patty claimed the mantle. I preferred the post and ironing board. We descended the stairs with our artifacts, realizing we were saying our final farewell to our beloved ancestors. We would not be visiting the place of our mother's birth together again.

Now Mom is in search of a new home. I know the move is uncomfortable for her also, but she has the courage to face the unknown—to move her emotional mantle. To leave the past behind and face a fresh future. If Mom is wired like her mom, she has enough juice running through her for another twenty years—and I like that.

My sisters and I will follow her to Florida. We will support her every step of her journey. Sure, there will be anxious times for us down the road, but Mom has taught us how to dismantle the fear of the unknown. She gives us courage to search for our mantle—to open the door of opportunity.

Yes, Mom is moving. Forward. Her roots will go down into Florida soil. She will build another mantle. For wherever Mom is, there is her mantle of love. And as always, that makes me feel secure, and a pill easier to swallow.

Napping in South Haven

Neusa, my young Brazilian friend, adopted me as one of her American moms almost immediately after I met her three months ago at work. Having left home two years ago to pursue her dreams, she has been granted several "moms" along her journey who offered love and support in a strange land. It is my blessing to be among them.

Neusa's kindness extended an invitation to me to meet her *real* mother during her first visit to the United States. After listening to Neusa's endearing stories of her mother, I was looking forward to making Madelena's acquaintance. Any mother of ten children has my respect.

Our destination was Lake Michigan for Madelena's first visit to a lakeshore. Kalamazoo was a stopover to meet a young man Neusa has been dating. After we enjoyed a Brazilian dish prepared by mother and daughter, we drove into town to find a place to celebrate life. Neusa strolled the summer streets holding her mom's hand, talking and translating Portuguese to keep the four of us laughing.

After a good night's rest (on a bachelor's sleeper sofa), we drove Saturday morning to South Haven to soak up the sun on Lake Michigan's sandy shore. Ah ... was I ready for some rest and recreation! I had not been to the beach this summer. And it was the perfect day. Not too hot or humid.

My white skin glowed in contrast to Neusa's beautiful brown body. I had to laugh at myself. Neusa has a way of making me feel young and unselfconscious. She taught me how to dive like a dolphin.

From the beach, I watched Neusa and her mother splash and dunk each other. I heard their laughter. Daughter gave mother swimming lessons as roles reversed once again in life's cycle. Goodness and mercy played before me uninhibited in waves of cool refreshment.

After lunch we sought a shady spot on thick grass by the channel leading into Lake Michigan. We spread out our towels once again, but this time we caught some z's for a summer's afternoon nap.

As I hovered in that mysterious place between the subconscious and conscious, sounds of life blew over me in gentle breezes. The motors of the boats idling through the channel mingled with human and animal voices. I had not found such relaxation in months.

A mother's voice fell upon my eavesdropping ears, "Why am I always the one who has to hold all the stuff?"

"Because you're the mom," was the spontaneous reply from a boy.

The protest was silenced.

It's that simple, isn't it? Mothers are made to bear burdens.

But the day will come when the roles will change and the boy will care for his mother. Just like Neusa taught her mother how to play in the water, so will the boy return to his mother what she has given him.

For we can't give without receiving. We can't lose without gaining. We don't always receive from the hand we have served, but be sure a pure heart will be rewarded.

I received the goodness Madelena gave Neusa. I lost my Becky two years ago, but gained Neusa. And in that blessing I find rest.

Just Aunt Jemima

September 9, 1998

Howdy, my name is Aunt Jemima. Back in 1945, Sadie McCoy's Aunt Pearl wrapped me up and gave me to Sadie for a weddin' gift. Aunt Pearl and Sadie were best friends growin' up, bein' birthed only three days apart. And Aunt Pearl, bein' larger than Sadie, protected her from bullies durin' recess. That made them real close.

So, it was only nat'ral for Aunt Pearl to give Sadie a real McCoy, of the pottery kind, to hold cookies in hopes to put some meat on Sadie's bones. Back then, my red kerchief and black face and hands were spankin' new. My big smile was real invitin' to those hankerin' for somethin' sweet.

And Sadie kept my wide skirt sittin' on her kitchen counter, full of cookies for her husban' and five girls. It was so funny how those chilin' would sneak into the kitchen, lift my big bosom so careful like, so'ins they wouldn't make no noise for Sadie to hear, and try to steal a cookie. I swar I never intended to snitch on those girls, but Sadie had a sense when their little hands were into mischief!

I still can't figure how she could hear me rattlin' through walls and floors! She'd yell, "Who's in the cookie jar?" Those little hands would drop me as fast as they could before Sadie found them out. It's a miracle I ain't been broke into pieces!

Yep, I saw many cookies come and go in them days. But after the girls grew up and left home, I sat with Sadie's other special things on a kitchen cabinet. Then a few years ago Sadie promised me to Iris, one of her daughters. I liked the idea of bein' full of cookies again and waited to be taken down from the shelf. But I wasn't purdy no more and didn't think Iris would want me. My smile was worn off from the kids handlin' me.

Well, Aunt Pearl is gone now and Sadie can't take me with her to her new home in Florida. So Iris wrapped me up a few weeks ago and moved me to her house. I didn't know what she saw in me. But it tickled me that she liked me the way I am, with chips, cracks and all!

When we got home, Iris carried her modern cookie jar to the basement, gave me a good washin' and put me on her kitchen counter. There aren't as many cookies comin' and goin' as the olden days cuz Iris's girls are all growed up too. But Ruth, Iris's youngin', likes to bake and filled my skirt with chocolate chip cookies.

It's funny. Iris called me an *icon* the other day when she took a cookie. I couldn't help but smile in spite of myself. I'm not sure what an *icon* is, but I have a feelin' it's something important. And that makes me laugh. Doesn't she know I'm just ol' Aunt Jemima? When my skirt is empty, no body comes 'round. But when I'm full, ever'body comes real close.

Joe, from Out of the Blue
and Philadelphia Too

September 11, 1998

Mega-stores make me nervous. The environment is unfriendly—the personal touch gets lost in the high and wide-open spaces. I boycott the big chains and shop small mom-and-pop places as often as time and finances permit. So, chances are I probably never would have entered Wal-Mart's doors if my painter, Cheryl, had not recommended Wal-Mart's paint (for the present project underway in my up-side-down house).

I anticipated a long search for a willing and capable sales person in the paint department. My former experience in such retail stores gave me legitimate reason for my attitude. But within minutes, I spied a man wearing a Wal-Mart vest. The paint splatters on the blue fabric gave a clue he was the one who could help me.

He responded with an eager yes when I approached him. I followed him a few feet to the paint counter, explaining my intentions and giving him my color samples. Remarkably friendly and knowledgeable of the products I needed, he removed the paint cans from the shelves and prepared to mix the paint.

As we chatted, out of the blue he asked if I worked in radio or television. He caught me by surprise. Was this a compliment or an accusation? I answered no, but I have considered radio from time to time. "What makes you ask?" I wondered out loud.

"Because you look like you belong on television," he said with all the confidence of a critic.

I argued, using my age as the obstacle to such a possibility. He returned with an optimistic gleam from his dark eyes, "Oh, I get tired of hearing that! We baby-boomers are just entering our prime."

Then clarifying I *do* work in communications, his eyes flashed again with, "I knew it! What kind of communications?"

His questions continued when I told him I was a writer. He confessed he once wrote a television script but was too afraid of rejection to submit it. We both agreed that fear is our worst enemy. He asked if I was ever going to write a novel.

"Someday," I said, "but I have to finish college first."

We exchanged names as we became acquainted. Joe and his Puerto Rican family moved to Michigan from Philadelphia in the late '80s. He has dreams of becoming a writer—of going back to school once he works out some financial details.

Assuring him he would achieve his dreams in time, his eyes quickened again when I added, "Most successful writers were once starving artists!"

He laughed, put both hands together, pointed to me, and nodded his head in rhythm with his Philly accent, "I like that ... artist."

"Yeah," I sighed, "but it's the starving part none of us like."

I sensed Joe's eyes saw something in me I didn't see. He seemed to believe more in my potential than I did.

And I have a hunch I saw something in him he didn't see. As he stood behind the paint counter and designed encouragement, I saw an artist inside the Wal-Mart vest. Like a fresh coat of paint renews a room, so does the application of encouragement from a pure heart upon another. To give someone the faith and courage needed to see themselves in a fresh perspective is truly the work of an artist.

The Parachute Story

October 16, 1998

I have always loved to listen to Mom tell stories, especially those that make her laugh when she tells them. The older we grow, the richer her Appalachia stories become to us both. I consume Mom's stories like her good Southern home cooking, savoring the flavor of congenial company long after the meal.

During a recent telephone call, Mom told me a story about a childhood friend, Victoria Miller. "Vickie" and Mom's younger sister, Sarah, were best friends. When Sarah died at age fourteen, their common loss bonded them in friendship: the kind that endures hardship.

It was in the middle of hard-times during WWII when Mom and Vickie were young women. Appalachian Kentucky severely felt the lack of resources for daily living. Mountain roads and a poor economy prevented the flow of household goods from city to country. Not only was food scarce, but clothing was a rare commodity. Silk stockings were a luxury and prized by women who possessed them. A new dress was not even a consideration. In country stores throughout the region, bolts of fabric gathered dust as retailers waited for the War to end.

Nevertheless, Vickie couldn't wait. She was planning a wedding. Her boyfriend was returning from the War. What was she going to do without money to buy material for her wedding dress?

In a stroke of invention and inspiration, Vickie and Mom unfolded the nylon parachute her boyfriend had mailed her from his wartime post. Vickie's little house looked like her lover had landed in the living room! It took some ingenuity and a great deal of perseverance to pin the pattern to the slippery fabric. They cut the parachute into pieces, and sewed them together. The finished product was a lovely dress.

Mom told me the story in just a few minutes without knowledge of how or why Vickie's boyfriend sent her the parachute. She delighted in the memory of making a wedding dress out of a parachute. That was all that mattered to her.

And that's all that mattered to me, for I heard her laugh again as I imagined Vickie walking down the aisle of a modest mountain church. I could hear Vickie's shoes striking the bare wooden floor as she approached the young man she loved. And the swooshing and swishing of her nylon dress turned everyone's head as she entered the door to the piano playing "Here Comes the Bride." The wafting fragrance of the white dogwood blossoms she held in her hands mingled with the mountain air in celebration over the congregation. It was a triumphant moment for Mom as she turned to the bride in admiration, feeling such a part of the event as she does even to this day.

Now the story is a part of me. My imagination digested another slice of Mom's life, making her more a part of my human spirit. That's how stories are. They are living things that teach us about who we are and how we became who we are.

Mom's story explains her "use what you have" model during the costly and demanding years of raising her five daughters. Time and time again, like a magician, she produced prom dresses from almost nothing. My sisters and I always left the house looking and feeling like princesses.

Indeed, Mom used what she had to sew the fabric of my life with the strong threads of resourcefulness. At times, all she had was a simple story of encouragement—a story of faith, hope and love.

Ultimately, that was and is enough for me. For nothing has fed and clothed my daughters and me like Mom's stories and laughter. And of course, when it comes to stories, Mom always has more than enough material to spin a good tale.

Lifesavers

October 23, 1998

I saw the bag of lifesavers hanging by the check-out counter as I stood ready to pay the Staples cashier for my report covers and Post-it page markers. The bag of individually wrapped lifesavers gave testimony of time and progress. Lifesavers are no longer just rolls and rings.

My mouth watered in response to the flavors the bright colors represented on the package. Grape. I love grape. Cherry too. They begged to be bought.

I didn't want to be late, so I grabbed the bag after a moment of mental debate. The lifesavers could possibly provide a topic for my creative writing workshop. I paid the bill and was on my way.

Later, when I unzipped my book-bag-on-wheels, removed the package of lifesavers and offered it to my class, a flood of flavors filled the room. Butterscotch memories resurrected taste buds long forgotten.

Mrs. Urban was my Sunday-school teacher when I was, oh, nine or ten. After she taught my class, she invited those of us who didn't have church-going parents to sit with her during the church service. It was her habit to pass a roll of butterscotch lifesavers to pacify us during an enthusiastic sermon by Reverend Sorrell.

My little heart, soul and mind were grounded in the Christian faith as the butterscotch ring melted in my mouth. Mrs. Urban offered me safety and salvation on Sunday mornings, and I accepted gratefully. Much older now, I realize I made steadfast decisions and commitments because of her charity. I wanted to be a Christian just like her.

Blessed is the child who is rescued by a lifesaver, to have a helping hand extended when in need, a shoulder to cry on when hurting. Quietly building character and virtue into the child's soul, most lifesavers go unnoticed until the child has grown and the lifesaver has gone to meet their Maker. Such is the case with Mrs. Urban. She received no reward from me, but I am confident she has embraced her glory nonetheless.

Thankfully, many of my lifesavers still dwell in their mortal bodies. Like my Aunt Dean, for example. She continues to influence my life with her gentle spirit as she has from the day I was born. Pure in heart and mind, she mentors me unaware, living simply and abundantly.

Aunt Dean loves me intensely. I know so because she has told me so all my life, and she gave me a roll of lifesavers upon my most recent visit with her. Isn't it peculiar? The cinnamon lifesavers (with no hole) moved me to reflection and gratification more than the $50 she placed in my hand for my fiftieth birthday.

To be sure, life could have made me hard-hearted and bitter if it had not been for the sweetness of my little lifesavers. Instead, the lingering butterscotch flavor developed a longing to be like Mrs. Urban and Aunt Dean: charitable, forgiving, gentle and dependable. And above all, to be a lifesaver.

Epilogue

Life is funny. You know what I mean—the paradoxes that stop us in our tracks and cause a pause midstream in our rush and routine.

For instance, here I am in the same small room Dad, Becky and Kelly once occupied. But Dad still smiles down at me while I compose at my computer. He is young, dressed in his Marine uniform, framed next to Mom in her 1940s pin-curled coiffure. Inscribed on the bottom right corner is "*To: Dad, the most wonderful man in the world. Your baby, Sadie Lee.*"

Even though Mom and Dad divorced in 1967, they remain inseparable. Even though the memories of paternal rejection and shame outnumber those of acceptance and love, they do not dominate. Even though we buried Dad's mortal body in the cold earth over five years ago, he lives in the warmth of my heart and home.

And to make life (and death) more peculiar, our Becky's grave is just yards south of her grandfather's. It's as if Becky made a statement in her burial—she was one step further toward the Homeplace where she longed to connect with her Nana and her roots.

At this moment, Becky radiantly smiles at me, peeking around the right side of my computer screen. Her memorial card is my constant companion, ever reminding me to love and play while there is life and breath. She helps me to unlearn lies and recognize the truth—to embrace the real issues of life. I weep and think again, *I would give anything to hear her voice and touch her face.* Some things never change. Yet, *I* have changed. Contradicting my Christian beliefs, my mother's heart finally understands why the bereaved consult psychics for one last contact with their beloved.

Paradoxes. Change and sameness dwell entwined within the soul, home, world and universe. My small room has been converted from Kelly's room dancing with tap shoes and other childhood memorabilia to a writer's haven, furnished with desk, file cabinets, computer system and fax machine. Kelly's childhood is packed away in her cedar chest, awaiting her retrieval. Her bed now accommodates guests in our basement. The passage into the empty nest and writer's life is fully accomplished.

And just when Mel, Ruth and I were making plans to visit Kelly in California for Thanksgiving, Kelly called to tell us that she's coming home. Although she loves San Francisco, she believes they are no longer meant for each other. (I never did adjust to the distance between California and Michigan.)

Yep, SF is out of her system, she said. Can you imagine my joy? Then came the addendum. Her return and residence will be only for a season. She desires to reconnect with her family before she sails the seas on another missionary journey. Where? Africa. She's finally reaching for her dream, her personal mission.

As I write, Kelly's making plans for our journey from Paradise to the Rust Belt (as she calls CA and MI respectively). I am thrilled to be her designated travel companion. One-on-one time with "Kell" for seven days (before she returns to the schemes of her sister, Ruth) should provide the best preparation for her next exodus from our family.

And just what does Ruth have up her sleeves these days? She's presently on the inside of the revolving door we call home and in happy pursuit of a "cool" place to rent with her sister. (Our voicemail greeting says, "This is the home of Mel and Iris Underwood, and sometimes Ruth".) With her bachelor's degree secured, she longs for the activity of the city's cultural center where she can satisfy her artistic appetites outside of her corporate profile. That's my eclectic and mercurial baby. Inch by inch, she shares her dreams with me over lunchtime soups and gingersnap cookies. We are learning to *"Tread softly because you tread on my dreams"* (William Butler Yeats). I can hardly contain my joy.

Yes, life is funny. Ruth, now older and wiser, finds certain qualities in her older sister that were once tiresome and disagreeable differences. Indeed, the distance between Kelly and Ruth is narrower these days. They long for the bond of sisterhood. They long to reunite with their Nana and Grandpa and Grandma Underwood. And this makes my heart glad.

And it makes my heart glad that Mel, Kelly, Ruth and I are traveling south together to the McCoy Bottom this Thanksgiving. You see, my mother returned her mantle to the Homeplace a year ago. Florida just wasn't her home. Her home is in the hills and hollers with Uncle Herm and Aunt Dean.

And it makes my heart glad that Mel and I have a home for our children to return to. A place to perpetuate the rituals and traditions of family and love. Hopefully, someday Kelly and Ruth will swing through our revolving door once more with husbands and babies in tow. But regardless of what the future holds, we will always speak of the legacies left before us. For in those legacies of happiness and hardships we find encouragement, passed down like precious treasures wrapped in embroidered cloth.

O dear reader, regard your treasure with care. Unwrap each deed and word in its season. Pause long enough in the fierce currents of life to embrace each moment of love and truth.

And in doing so, please remember my Becky. In the immutable seasons of life, may you remember there will always be a Becky.

To order *Encouraging Words for All Seasons*, cut on the dotted line and mail the order form with a check of $15.50 ($13.95 plus $1.55 shipping and handling) per copy payable to Iris Lee Underwood to the following address:

>ArtLee Communications
>960 Yule Road
>Leonard, Michigan 48367

Or order by email at **iris@irislee.org**

....

Enclosed is $_____ for _____ copies of *Encouraging Words for All Seasons*.

Please mail to:

_____ (name)
_____ (street, apt. #)
_____ (city, state, zip code)
_____ (country)

Printed in the United States
40549LVS00001B/103-132

9 781587 360169